65
SUCCESSFUL
HARVARD
BUSINESS SCHOOL
APPLICATION
ESSAYS

65 SUCCESSFUL HARVARD BUSINESS SCHOOL APPLICATION ESSAYS

The Staff of the *Harbus*,
the Harvard Business School Student Newspaper

ST. MARTIN'S GRIFFIN ❧ NEW YORK

www.stmartins.com

Library of Congress Cataloging-in-Publication Data

65 successful Harvard Business School application essays, with analysis by the staff of
    The Harbus, the newspaper of Harvard Business School / Dan Erck, Pavel Swiatek, and
    members of the Harbus staff.
        p. cm.
    ISBN 0-312-33448-6
    EAN 978-0312-33448-2
        1. Business schools—United States—Admission. 2. Exposition (Rhetoric)
    3. Essay—Authorship. 4. Business writing. 5. Harvard Business School.
    I. Title: Sixty-five successful Harvard Business School application essays.
    II. Title: Harvard Business School application essays. III. Erck, Dan. IV. Swiatek,
    Pavel. V. Harbus.

    HF1131.A135 2004
    808'06665—dc22

                                                                            2004049743

10 9 8 7 6 5

CONTENTS

Contents

Contents

VI. THREE ACCOMPLISHMENTS

VII. STRENGTHS AND WEAKNESSES

VIII. WHY DO YOU NEED AN HBS MBA?

Contents

IX. OPTIONAL ESSAY

ACKNOWLEDGMENTS

The inspiration for this book came from Pawel Swiatek, Harvard Business School Class of 2004 and a graduate of Harvard College. Pawel was familiar with a book of essays published by the *Harvard Crimson*, the undergraduate daily student newspaper, and suggested the *Harbus*, the HBS weekly student newspaper, undertake a similar project.

It is worth noting this book is created by the Harbus News Corporation, an independent nonprofit entity, not the Harvard Business School. The *Harbus* contributes its profits to a grant-making foundation that supports community organizations and schools in the Boston area.

The views and opinions expressed in this book do not necessarily reflect those of the Harvard Business School and the references to the school throughout the book do not mean that the school endorses these views or opinions.

A huge debt of thanks is owed to six contributors from the Class of 2005 who helped select essays and write the critiques and chapter introductions: Analisa Balares, LaMonica Carpenter, Sara Cherlin, Jamyn Edis, Ling Hu, and Valerie Valtz. We would also like to thank the staff of the *Harbus*, including Keith Wolf, Kate Eberle, Meg Dolan, and Jenny Schultz. Lastly, we would be remiss if we did not express our gratitude for assistance from our agent, Linda Mead, and our editor at St. Martin's, Ethan Friedman.

INTRODUCTION

We cannot promise you that if you buy this book you will definitely get in to Harvard Business School. There are some books and Web sites out there that guarantee such things; we do not. That is in part why you should read this book: we are being honest with you.

This book is not about foolproof recipes for admission. It is not about insider tricks that you can use to beat the system. It is, however, about inspiring you to write great essays and showing you that there is no one right way to answer any of the application questions. HBS, like most top business schools, is a remarkably diverse place. In each section of around ninety students there are on average people from close to thirty countries. Beyond geographic diversity, there are of course bankers and consultants, but also doctors and lawyers, fighter pilots and teachers, writers and athletes. We tried to reflect this highly intentional diversity among students by including a broad range of writing styles and essay responses in this book. Our intent is to demystify one of the many parts of the admissions process by showing you a variety of essays that were successful. There are dozens of ways to address each application question and our goal here is to provide a sample of what has worked in the past. The magic formula is that there is no magic formula. Be yourself. Be honest. Be thoughtful. Reveal who you really are and how you approach problems. Tell the admissions committee why you are you.

At first glance, you may be tempted to think that there is nothing sufficiently unique about you to make yourself stand out from a crowd of candidates. After all, HBS receives some nine thousand applications in an average year. The examples included in this volume will hopefully save you from this temptation. While some of the essays do describe amazing experiences, many others focus on everyday, perhaps even pedestrian subjects. But when they do, they do so in an extraordinary way. The critical point to understand is that the anecdotes are never an end in and of themselves. They are a tool for conveying your personality, values, self-awareness, maturity, leadership skills, sense of humor, and all the other qualities that will contribute to your success at business school. Even the most exotic accomplishment will be ineffective in an essay that fails to explain what you learned, how you changed, and why it was important. On the other hand, seemingly unremarkable activities such as a morning jog or staring out of a taxicab window can provide the perfect setting for demonstrating key aspects of your personality or explaining how you have come to set your life's goals.

If you spend enough time thinking about all the different experiences and influences that have shaped you, you are likely to come up with far more than you could possibly fit into the application. Ideally, you would include them all, but given the space constraints you will have to choose the most important ones. Make a list (even if it is only a mental one) and begin mapping out your six or seven essays. While you may thread some common overarching themes through all of them, each one ought to provide a unique insight into what makes you tick and how you approach your life, your family, your career, and your education (to name but a few relevant subjects). Because space is at such a premium, make sure you avoid repetition. For instance, if you show how you proved yourself as a competent manager in one essay, use another one to discuss a deeply personal issue, such as your relationship with your siblings. The more aspects of your personality you share, the better the admissions committee will be able to get to know you. Your ultimate goal is to portray yourself as more than just a candidate represented by the résumé, the transcript, and the GMAT scores. While those elements of your application are also quite important, the essays give you a chance to show that you are an individual who will be a strong contributor to the HBS community in the classroom and far beyond.

Once you map out the general content of your essays, you will face the next hurdle: the word limit. Is it really possible to say anything deep in three hundred words? The essays included in this volume will hopefully be sufficient to convince you that it is. Three hundred words actually provide plenty of space to say (and imply) a great deal about you. Our recommendation (but by no means the only way to tackle this problem) is to draft each essay as if the word limit did not exist, and only then pare it down to size. The process will force you to ask yourself repeatedly: "What am I *really* trying to say here? What is my *core* message?" This way, you will weed out excessive descriptions and irrelevant details and be left with a clear, focused, and succinct essay.

Also, remember that you are writing essays for business school; if your writing is beautiful and polished, it will most certainly help. But do not lose sleep trying to win a Pulitzer. Substance is what really counts here.

Finally, a word of caution: while it is obvious that you should not copy the essays included in this book, you also should not even use them as direct models or outlines for your own work. You will be caught plagiarizing and your effort will be for naught. You are busy and so is the admissions committee; do not waste your time or theirs.

Start by reading the sixty-five essays that follow. We think they are excellent examples. But they are only that: examples. They are indicative of the level of depth and introspection you need to achieve. In order to succeed, you will need to write about you. So

Introduction

take a deep breath, try to relax (knowing that might be hard), and verbalize what makes you a unique candidate.

Best of luck,

Dan Erck and Pawel Swiatek

Harvard Business School Class of 2004

On behalf of the Harbus News Corporation

I. BEING A LEADER

Choose a recent experience in which you acted as a leader. Briefly outline the situation, describe your leadership role, and then explain how you were effective and what you learned.

Discuss an experience that has had an impact on your development as a leader.

Before responding to one of the above essay topics, you must decide on your own conception of leadership. It's not equivalent to basic management skills, nor is it rooted in issuing orders. In fact, the more you think about it, the harder it becomes to pin down a single definition. As you comb through your life experiences, you will discover that your leadership skills appear in multiple contexts and take many different forms.

The following essays illustrate this diversity. For some of the authors, leadership takes place in the context of teamwork. For others, it manifests itself in guiding organizational change. In one of the essays, it takes the shape of quick decision-making that impacts the lives of subordinates.

Many applicants have trouble identifying their leadership experiences. It is natural that most college graduates with a few years of work experience will not have run a division of a *Fortune* 500 company or eradicated a disease in the Amazon. This is to be expected. Leadership, however, does not require a grandiose setting. As the following examples prove, routine military exercises can provide as much of an opportunity as a college daily paper. Interacting with the school faculty may be as challenging as coordinating an international project in Africa or convincing a company to change the way it goes about product development.

The point of this essay topic is not to extract an exaggerated account of a large project where you ascribe all the credit to yourself. The intent is to elicit a description of an experience where your thoughts and actions brought about a result that would not have happened in your absence. The result itself, however, is less important than what you have taken away from the experience. While leadership may be hard to define, practicing it requires constant learning through introspective analysis. It is this ability that you need to emphasize through your well-chosen example. In order to make a lasting impression, your essay must paint a clear picture of what your conception of leadership is, how you practice it, and how you think about improving your command of this elusive skill.

—Pawel Swiatek

Chris Howard

There are over ten million children orphaned by HIV/AIDS living in sub-Saharan Africa. I met several last year during my visit to Gaborone, Botswana—Phangisilie, Grace, and Joseph to name but a few. They, along with the other four hundred children at the Mpule Kwelegobe Center for Children, will at least have access to care as a result of the efforts of an unlikely collaboration between businesspeople and artists whom I led over a six-month period.

I joined Bristol-Myers Squibb (BMS) to serve as an international project manager on Secure the Future, a $100 million five-year program that provides care and support for women and children with HIV/AIDS in five southern African countries, primarily through grants for medical research and community education. Among my first assignments was raising awareness and mobilizing resources for AIDS victims by using art. Developing a team of over thirty individuals from BMS, several African art galleries and museums, and our South African–based communications firm, we partnered with the Harvard AIDS Institute and the former Miss Universe, Mpule Kwelegobe, to create ArtWorks for AIDS. The exhibition included original commissioned pieces from more than thirty artists on the subject of HIV/AIDS, emphasizing the plight of women and children. ArtWorks premiered at the World Conference on AIDS in Durban just six months after it was conceived, toured several international venues, and earned close to $100,000 for AIDS orphans during an auction on November 30.

As the international project manager-leader, I was responsible for devising a vision and strategy for the project, assembling the team, establishing milestones, maintaining the budget, and delivering the art by the beginning of July. I was effective in this role for several reasons. First, I ensured that the *team*, rather than I alone, collectively devised a vision and timeline for the project by meeting with the key participants individually to better understand their ideas. We then conducted a brainstorming session where all involved parties freely expressed their ideas to the group. Thus, each team member could claim ownership in our success. Second, I was able to mitigate cultural differences between the southern African, northern European, and American participants because of my extensive study of and travel to both regions. Third, although I recognized that the team members from the art community did not necessarily subscribe to business principles, I never let them use it as an excuse for poor performance.

My key learning is somewhat simple but compelling nonetheless; anytime you create a team comprising parties who are naturally suspicious of one another, honesty is paramount. That's the only way I could get artists to trust and perform for businessmen and vice versa. I fostered this sense of trust by maintaining clear lines of communication between all parties as well as refusing to alter the mutually agreed upon project tenants just to suit the interests of whomever I was speaking with. The result was a stunning visual homage to the over twenty-four million people suffering from HIV/AIDS in Africa as well as additional care and support for hundreds of children in Botswana. But why don't you see for yourself . . . the Smithsonian purchased two of the works.

ANALYSIS

When reading Chris's essay, you may be tempted to assume that its success stems from the exceptional and highly laudable humanitarian nature of the project he describes. This is not the case. While his participation in ArtWorks for AIDS testifies to his commendable commitment to international development, it is not by itself sufficient to illustrate his leadership ability. Chris provides enough context to demonstrate the gravity of his project, but then devotes most of his essay to describing the challenges he faced as a project leader and the techniques he employed to overcome them.

Collaboration, consensus-building, and bridging cultural gaps might sound like vague abstractions elsewhere, but in this case they are specific illustrations of Chris's ability to lead a multinational, multicultural team of people with very diverse backgrounds. Without bragging, Chris proves his competence. Perhaps including a couple of brief but illustrative anectodes (while abbreviating the context description) would have made his account even more vibrant.

The concluding paragraph is the crowning touch. Chris shows that his very successful project was also a learning opportunity. No matter what types of projects he leads in the future, establishing trust and open communication between participants will be one of his priorities. Most certainly this will make him a more effective leader.

John Leroi

As managing editor of University of Michigan's student newspaper, I was responsible for deciding how to appropriately cover the football team's quest for its first national championship in over fifty years. I decided to publish a special edition on the afternoon of Michigan's final regular season game—but only if the team won. As managing editor, I led a team of reporters, editors, advertising managers, and circulation managers that successfully printed the first Saturday afternoon edition in the 107-year history of the *Michigan Daily*.

My greatest challenge was to align the separate staffs in one common vision. While the editorial staff was excited about the project, many advertising managers felt uncomfortable selling ads for a newspaper that may never get published. Likewise, the circulation department had qualms about distributing the newspapers when university buildings, our usual delivery points, were closed. I met with the leaders of each staff to discuss their concerns and gain a greater understanding of their operations. I evaluated various scenarios, and developed a plan in which editorial and business staffs would collaborate on circulation and advertising responsibilities. This not only alleviated concerns about a tight deadline, but also allowed sportswriters and advertising managers to collectively identify local merchants that would covet advertising space in this issue. Additionally, the circulation department worked with the arts and leisure staff to select local bars and restaurants as new delivery points.

Through this experience I learned to integrate disparate inputs into a unified perspective. Although very little can be accomplished without well-balanced, multidisciplined teams, molding different viewpoints into a single vision is a task that can trip up all but the most successful leaders. I've learned to request input from each team member, not because it is important to make them feel valuable, but because open discussion is the best way to generate successful ideas.

ANALYSIS

In recounting this episode in leadership experience, John highlights one of the biggest challenges facing the head of any organization: aligning disparate interests. He provides just enough detail to convey the complexity of the issues, ranging from advertising sales to distribution logistics, as well as the multitude of concerns among the different team members involved in a trailblazing, unorthodox project. There is no doubt that publishing the first Sunday edition was no easy feat, requiring all the negotiation and consensus-building skill he could muster.

However, this essay works not just because John provides an instance of visionary leadership or of leading his team to a common decision and a landmark execution. These elements are important, but not sufficient. The essay works because John shares his conclusions about what factors contribute to management success. His talent lies not in publishing a Sunday edition of a college daily, but in his understanding how to manage and motivate a large team—a skill applicable in a much broader context than the *Michigan Daily*. In other words, he demonstrates his potential for leadership in a business environment.

A minor addition that would have made this essay even more effective involves a change of sequence. Starting with a terse

I. Being A Leader

description of the management challenge would have added dynamism to the text and made the reader more curious about the context and the resolution. When competing with thousands of essays on the same topic, having an attention-grabbing first paragraph can constitute a major advantage.

KATY Y. HUANG

I was elected the first foreign chairman of the Oxford University engineering student board (ESB). My most difficult challenge was to convince the faculty to change the way our courses were taught. No former chairmen had attempted that successfully. Moreover, I had only one month to persuade them if changes were to be implemented for the following year. The curriculum assigned equal weighting and time to all courses. However, to learn effectively, we needed different time allocations. Politically, this was very sensitive, as faculty egos were at stake: more time might imply poor teaching and less time might imply less significance.

As I learned in organizational behavior classes, I appealed to the faculty rationally, emotionally, and through syndication. First, I led twenty committee members to carry out a comprehensive student survey. By working together, splitting the target group of 720 students between us, we achieved a record 80 percent response rate. Second, I focused the faculty, who were under pressure from the British government to improve teaching standards, on the bigger picture. I offered them a way to bring the students on board. Lastly, I spoke to all key faculty members, incorporated their feedback and briefed them on the results. Therefore, there were no surprises at the ESB meeting, the faculty accepted our recommendation, and it was implemented the following year.

I learned that with teamwork and individual accountability we accomplished a survey that decoupled the link between course importance and time allocation, which provided the most objective evidence for change. Emotionally, I empathized with the faculty and emphasized the need to improve our course. I compared us to other universities to avoid the personal "ego traps" within the department. Most importantly, syndication prior to the actual meeting ensured a successful conclusion.

ANALYSIS

Effecting change in an organization with historically established norms and procedures is tremendously challenging even for elected officers. Katy's description of the politically charged nature of the proposed changes makes success seem improbable. Nonetheless, she succeeds thanks to a structured, multifaceted leadership style. She guides her fellow students' survey effort and gingerly leads the faculty to a new, mutually beneficial solution. She is not a mere process manager, but a mediator who seeks to understand and clarify the rational and emotional motives of all the parties involved. This understanding enables her to build consensus and lead change.

The final agreement appears to be the inevitable result of her multiple initiatives, as if she had planned it down to the last detail. She establishes herself as a competent leader who instead of jumping into an unproductive confrontation takes time to analyze the situation, creates a detailed tactical plan, and then leads her supporters' efforts to produce the desired outcome. Her essay leaves no doubt about her broadly applicable ability to set a goal, secure a broad base of support, and then reach it.

While the text conveys the intended message quite well, the concluding paragraph could be improved with more synthesis of the lessons learned. The statements about "teamwork" and "individual accountability" do not reflect the profound understanding of practical leadership that Katy clearly possesses. A more general conclusion on leading change would have made this essay truly exceptional.

MICHAEL MUNSON

Traditionally, investment banks perform exhaustive financial due diligence to understand a company's prospects before accepting it as a client. During the technology boom of 1998–2000, the rules changed. Numerous early-stage telecommunications companies with almost no financial histories sought services from my group at Goldman Sachs. Bankers were suddenly thrust in the new position of evaluating businesses based upon unfamiliar technology distinctions. I struggled to grasp the significance of core technologies and discovered that many colleagues faced similar challenges.

In response, I decided to arrange a seminar that would teach telecom technology concepts. As an analyst, I could not alone receive the attention and support of my group's leaders. Therefore, I coordinated with peers to collectively pitch the proposal. Eventually, management supported the project and suggested that internal industry experts lead a seminar. I surveyed my peers to understand problem areas and developed a syllabus. Goldman's experts repeatedly cancelled the session, however, as they considered training a relatively low priority in the midst of the chaotic deal environment. After researching alternatives, I suggested that we set a firm date and hire external technology consultants to provide a more comprehensive, albeit costly, seminar. Management accepted this proposal and more than two hundred attendees from multiple investment banking groups attended the full day of training. According to colleagues' comments, the firm both targeted clients more carefully and advised them more intelligently as a result.

While selling this expensive alternative to group leaders, I learned the importance of building a coalition and articulating a proposal in appropriate terms. Management committed funds once I detailed how the training would help the firm win additional business and not serve merely as continuing education. I also learned that identifying a problem is not enough to contribute to an organization. Leadership requires persistence to develop and implement a solution in the face of institutional resistance.

ANALYSIS

Michael uses his essay to achieve three important goals.

First, he provides a vivid yet concise example of acting as a leader. The experience clearly demonstrates his ability to take initiative and push a project to completion. The details about building support lend credibility to the challenge and lend gravity to the effort.

Second, Michael demonstrates his understanding of leadership as a general concept. It is not enough to have a good idea. Being an effective leader requires building coalitions and overcoming institutional inertia. Poor communication can be deadly, as can be a lack of persistence or conviction. Successful leadership cannot be achieved alone.

Finally, and perhaps most importantly, Michael creates a seamless connection between a specific example and the abstract concept of leadership. The two parts of the essay are mutually reinforcing and help portray Michael as an effective yet thoughtful businessman.

This essay serves to highlight a small but important point about writing on leadership. Michael admits that the original proposition was "coordinated with peers." The phrase is dangerously ambiguous and the effort could be interpreted as something

I. Being A Leader

Michael was involved in, but not necessarily in a leadership role. Fortunately, the rest of the essay clearly shows him taking charge. Nonetheless, when writing your essay you should try to avoid such ambiguity.

JONATHAN SPIER

The market for my firm's software was hot, and engineering was racing to keep up with demand. Quality suffered. We could hand-hold customers through quality problems when we had three customers. Suddenly, we had three hundred.

For nine months, my team had struggled to support our new customers on a promising yet often unreliable product. I knew something needed to change. At the kickoff of our next release, I preached a new approach to our work. We needed to focus on quality, and we needed to make our product easier to use and maintain. The team voiced strong approval for my vision. Nothing changed.

Words alone were not enough. Change would require creativity and deliberate action on my part. I worked to develop procedures to change my group's culture. I built more time into project plans for testing. I implemented new quality measurements to quantify the coverage of our tests. I challenged the team to beat aggressive coverage targets in each project milestone. I added quality as a regular discussion item in weekly meetings and publicly recognized excellent efforts to improve reliability.

With constant reinforcement, the team culture shifted. In short time, the quality assurance department joked that my team was not producing enough bugs. Our chief architect held my project up at a manager's meeting as "an example of how projects at the company should be run." Senior management adopted my team's quality metrics as the standard for measuring quality for each group. Other managers who had originally questioned my plan to invest more engineering time in testing now began to imitate it.

A leader must understand where the company is, where it needs to be, and how the company culture needs to evolve to get it there. Through this experience, I learned that a leader cannot just preach a vision. A leader must initiate action to shape corporate culture and drive change.

ANALYSIS

Jonathan's essay is another example of leading change within an organization. Like the previous two authors, he shows that a clever idea by itself is insufficient to overcome ingrained organizational behavior. What makes the story unique, however, is his description of learning from failure. He is not ashamed to admit that his initial approach of "words alone" was ineffective. While someone else might have given up at that point, Jonathan escalated his commitment to change by taking specific and incremental steps. The essay portrays him as a flexible yet effective and committed leader, while the experience lends itself very nicely to his generalizations about leadership as a concept. The conclusion that leadership must be practiced every day and cannot be constrained to an abstract "vision" shows that Jonathan has learned a valuable lesson from this experience.

ARTHUR JOSEPH O'KEEFE IV

USS *Georgia* hurtled through the Pacific hundreds of feet below the surface, and I was at her helm as Officer of the Deck. Our submarine's massive battery was almost drained, common after a day of intense training, when I received an emergency report that a failed instrument had shut down the reactor. Without an operational reactor or fresh air for the diesel generator, the ship had to rely solely on its nearly depleted battery for electrical power. Unless I took decisive action, *Georgia* would go dead in the water. Consequently, I ordered all non-vital electrical loads switched off and turned my focus to driving our 18,000-ton warship to periscope depth to snorkel on the diesel.

The sonar team reported that they could hear numerous ships, so I conducted several tactical maneuvers to estimate range, course, and speed of each. The results were disconcerting. One ship was close, and it would take skill to avoid hitting it. With the battery quickly discharging though, I dared not wait to reevaluate. I chose a course and ordered the diving officer to bring the ship to periscope depth. As we came shallow, the diesel started, and the battery was unloaded. I peered out the periscope and watched a supertanker pass safely down our side.

As I coordinated the efforts of the crew to "fight the ship," I was invigorated. Performing a successful approach to periscope depth under these intense circumstances was deeply rewarding. Afterward, when I wondered why I felt excited rather than scared or upset, I realized that I thrive on working with a team to accomplish difficult goals and performing well in stressful situations.

ANALYSIS

In 272 words Arthur proves his competence as a leader. The first paragraph succinctly lays out the context and the challenge, while the second one describes the quick thinking behind the decision to surface the nuclear submarine. There is no doubt that Arthur is able to make difficult choices and take calculated risks under pressure. The final paragraph is essential to making this essay work. An adrenaline-filled moment is but a fleeting rush if it fails to inspire a certain degree of reflection. In this case, Arthur makes it clear that he evaluates such experiences ex post facto and through them learns about himself.

The essay also shows that leadership is not confined to managing teams or guiding organizations through change. Being entrusted with authority to make critical choices for others is an aspect of leadership not discussed by the preceding authors. Arthur leads by quickly making a difficult decision with potentially dire consequences that ultimately ascertains the survival of his ship and crew. His ability to handle (and even enjoy) the pressure attest to his leadership stamina.

This essay could benefit from a few additional details. For example, although Arthur mentions teamwork in his concluding sentence, his story does not convey much about the role of the crew in navigating this stressful situation. Also, a slightly longer description of the serious consequences of a wrong decision would further highlight the pressure he was facing. A concluding statement about leadership consisting of fast decision-making as well as guiding teams through difficult tasks would have added even more punch.

Anonymous

In late 1999, I was promoted to marketing director for Ford Turkey. My immediate task was to raise profitable market share in the short-term while improving the brand's image so as to propel sustainable future growth. Given the great freedom the position entailed, I was charged with conceiving and implementing plans to realize our sales targets.

Being effective required that I overcome three distinct challenges.

First, making the transition to marketing director demanded that I gain a firm grasp on all of the department's functions and ongoing projects very quickly. The combination of my analytical skills and ability to focus on multiple tasks simultaneously enabled me to expedite the transition process and become effective in my job almost immediately.

Second, because I was the youngest manager in the company, I had to gain the respect of and build a great rapport with staff. By utilizing my interpersonal skills and establishing weekly departmental meetings and social events, I earned the staff's trust through clearly communicating my vision for the department and providing a forum for their opinions, ideas, and concerns as well as infusing the department with greater "team spirit."

Third, I had to prepare for the imminent launch of two new cars. My strong negotiation skills enabled us to acquire the services of new, better advertising firms at half the previous cost. We also reformulated our brand communication strategy so as to create a unified message that encompassed all our products. The sum of the innovative approaches I led was an increase in overall market share from 5.5 percent to 7.7 percent in fewer than eighteen months and in spite of Turkey's ongoing financial crisis.

Besides confirming my confidence in my leadership skills and motivating my desire to reach a top-level executive position, this experience taught me that the key to success is setting high goals while conveying the belief that they are attainable. Additionally, I learned that managers must trust and act upon their intuition when a situation calls for urgent action.

ANALYSIS

Even though this essay has nothing to do with saving the world or averting disaster it serves as a very good illustration of the author's leadership abilities. The context is a job promotion—an event relatively common among applicants. Without dwelling on the promotion itself (which is an achievement, but does not necessarily prove anything about leadership potential), the author demonstrates his aptitude by identifying particular managerial challenges and describing his ability to overcome them efficiently. The author explains how he applied specific skills (analytical, communications, interpersonal, etc.) to establish his credibility and to reach quantifiable results. It is clear that throughout this experience, he and his team faced significant barriers, but thanks to his actions managed to overcome them successfully.

The lessons that conclude the essay are a good attempt at incorporating a touch of introspection. In this case, however, they seem somewhat disconnected from the body of the essay. A tighter logical connection between the challenges and the lessons would have truly completed this essay.

Jannike Aase

In investment banking, projects are executed in small, hierarchical teams. The analyst, the most junior member of the team, is not expected to be a leader. In my experience, however, taking leadership is a personal choice that is not discouraged by the rigid team structure, as the following recent example will show.

The intense project had only four days left to an important client board meeting as I learned that the associate on my team had just been asked to resign, due to the worsening market conditions. She had been in control of the forthcoming presentation and was my closest supervisor on the team. Sad for my colleague and friend, I also feared the project would suffer greatly, and informed the vice president on the team that we needed reinforcements.

Realizing that I probably had the best understanding of the process after this, I took on a leadership role on the project. I walked the team through the financial model and the presentation draft, explaining the assumptions taken, suggested new analysis to conduct and at one point persuaded the team that a proposed analysis would not add sufficient value to the presentation. I made certain we talked to the relevant people to complete our qualitative analysis, and suggested a way to split the work between us. After the client meeting, the senior team members informed me that they appreciated my leadership in the project, driving both the qualitative and the quantitative analysis forward.

In former leadership experiences I have always held a well-defined, formal leadership position, either, for instance, in the form of being a platoon leader or in the form of being the leader of the student teaching evaluation board. Through this experience and similar situations I have learned that leadership more often than not is something you assume, not something that is handed to you. By taking initiative and being proactive I can lead my project or parts of my projects towards a successful completion.

ANALYSIS

This transformational essay could just as easily fall under the defining moment category but serves its purpose well as an example of a young person, in this case an analyst at a bank, learning to act as a leader. Jannike faces a situation common to many applicants, especially in recent years: her boss has been fired and she has to figure out how to pick up the slack to prepare for an important presentation. What sets this essay apart from others is not the description of the problem. Rather, it is what Jannike learns from the experience. Specifically, she takes her previous conception of leadership (based on a well-defined role in an organization) and describes how that view has changed as a result of her experience at the bank. Her conclusion is that taking initiative is more important than your title or formal role in an organization. Jannike presents herself as someone who is comfortable leading projects and who would thrive both at HBS and in her career to follow.

The one thing that could have improved Jannike's essay would be getting to the point a little faster in the first paragraph. Given the tight word limit it is important to grab the reader in the first sentence or two. In this case, Jannike is trying to set the stage by showing how she acted as a leader in a situation where she was not expected to be one. That comes across clearly as the essay unfolds and as a result makes the first paragraph somewhat unnecessary. With a limited word count at your disposal, make every sentence meaningful.

II. A TYPICAL DAY

While recognizing that no day is typical, describe a representative day.

This is an essay question that at first glance seems almost too easy: describe a typical day. How hard can that be? Do not be fooled: this is a question worth spending some time on and one that if done well can communicate a great deal about your personality and how you approach the world and solve problems.

The chronology of what you do and the hour-by-hour specifics of your diary are not all that important. What matters here is how you choose to say what you say. To simply list what you do is not going to win you many points. Your résumé probably covers most of what you do (or should, anyway) so this is your chance to demonstrate why you are good at what you do and what types of experiences you will contribute as a member of the HBS community.

As you will see from the essays we have chosen, there are many approaches that can work. Bending the rules with this essay is okay, so do not feel compelled to describe your day purely chronologically. Many people, though, do exactly that, so if that is how you end up approaching the essay that is fine.

In addition to showing a range of formats that can work, we have tried to pick essays that are especially good at revealing aspects of the author's character and personality. Some are funny but many are not. Some are strikingly well written but, again, many are not. Writing beautifully helps (sometimes a lot) but it is not a prerequisite for admission. What is? The ability to demonstrate perspective, poise, and maturity, all of which are common to all the essays we have chosen.

Most people who apply have done interesting and important things, so simply confirming or reiterating that you too have done interesting and important things is not going to distinguish you from the crowd. The key here is not to underestimate what seems like an overly easy question. This is an additional opportunity to help the admissions committee learn more about you and how you view the world.

—Dan Erck

ANONYMOUS

Alarm clock. Clock radio. Cereal. Multivitamin. Rain. No jog today.

The firm represents your career as one pyramid inverted on top of the other. The bottom pyramid represents analysts and associates; the top pyramid, junior and senior partners. At the fulcrum is the case manager. It is the best and worst role at the firm.

Five new voice mails, 12 new e-mails. Scan *Red Herring*, *Venture Wire*, *American Banker*, *WSJ*, and the *NY Times*. Must stay current, I rationalize. Client calls. "Could we have an update before the presentation to review the findings?" The presentation is only four days away. "Absolutely." "I'll see you tomorrow in Parsippany at eight-thirty A.M."

The best part is that you see and do it all. You watch partners agree to outrageous proposals. You design the analysis to execute those proposals. You learn your clients' quirks and earn their confidence. You guide your team. You support the firm, too—writing articles, giving recruiting seminars on "cracking a case interview."

A partner stops by: "I promised Tom that we would incorporate the perspective of Japanese beverage executives." Panic. The analyst reminds you of his vacation. Meet with case team. Reshuffle work plan. Interview client CFO. Rewrite executive summary (again). Gently, have "career concerns" discussion with advisee.

The worst part is that you see and do it all. It is all ultimately your responsibility: the right answer, a happy client, a non-mutinous case team, the partner appearing at the meeting and remembering the topic. You are one part uber-analyst, one part therapist, one part administrative assistant. Secretly, I like this responsibility, too.

What time does the gym close? Business plan needs another iteration. Girlfriend calls: "We are meeting for dinner at nine, right?" Panic. E-mail document to client. Grab a taxi. Rain. Everything will be fine. It always is.

ANALYSIS

If you are a consultant, answering this question can be terrifying. Everyone knows what a consultant does but here you are trying to describe a typical day in a way that is interesting and that sets you apart from the crowd. It is no easy task, but the writer of this essay passes with flying colors.

Humor helps, as does the author's thoughtful (and honest) perspective of what it is like to be a case manager and balance the myriad demands from coworkers, partners, clients, and life outside of work. The writing is crisp and the pace fast. The end of the essay—"Everything will be fine. It always is."—is a nice touch and says to the admissions committee that the author is not so overwhelmed by day-to-day pressures that he loses sight of the bigger picture and what is really important in life. No matter what your background, demonstrating that you can see your job in a larger context (connecting the dots, so to speak) is invaluable and demonstrates maturity and poise. The takeaway from this essay is that you can do a lot with three hundred words. Do not panic if you are worried you are not an amazing writer but do spend the time to think about what it is that you do, why you do it well, and how you can convey that and a bit about your personality in as short a space as possible.

ADRIAN BLAIR

My run ends on Parliament Hill; through mist I pick out a beautiful, distant dome—St. Paul's. Suffocating subway journey crushes the inspiration; people become silent, menacing competitors for space. Humanity revived by brief exchange of funny faces with a bored child.

Immediate interrogation by Françoise, our receptionist, for post-party gossip; we laugh as I promise full disclosure later. Skim through industry newsletters. Alta Vista in trouble; Streetmap, an important partner, moving into mobile. Call friends at both with ideas on working together. 9:30—a session with our marketing and sales directors, on developing a "money channel." I'm skeptical. Can we really improve on existing services? We discuss my concerns about this, its fit with our brand values, and its impact on current finance partners. A fascinating session. Then I probe specifics. What additional work is required? Who will do what, by when?

Back to four voice mails from companies wanting to work with us. Call each back, hoping for that rare gem of an idea; form rapid judgments. Choose one for further analysis in my weekly "new ideas review."

Quick sandwich, then see the MD of BeFree, our affiliate program technology partner. I outline three aims for the 2002 contract. He's baffled when I talk about reducing the burden on Kerneena in our finance team before I mention pricing. Then to concierge services provider TenUK—we're excited about plans to unlock the revenue potential of a Jeeves-branded concierge service—our first wholly "off-line" project.

No meetings after 6:00. I study the *Economist* "mobile internet" survey—an area I'm keen to bring Ask Jeeves closer to. Research some suppliers before I shut down. Reflect on the day. Where should the company be going? Will everything I did today help us get there?

Then a different world. The London debut of Nadia Cole, a young Canadian pianist. Still can't agree with my musical friends on the merits of her Liszt. . . .

ANALYSIS

The pace in this essay is frenetic and the language clipped. "Alta Vista in trouble," for example, could probably benefit from a verb. So could other sentences. Never mind, there is no time. Work is moving too quickly to bother. Such is life on Internet time. Adrian could come across as rushed but instead manages to seem thoughtful. He frames his day nicely and in the first paragraph makes the point that yes, he is busy but not too busy to miss the beauty of the dome of St. Paul's or to take joy from making funny faces with a child on the subway. The ending is cliché (contrasting working at an Internet start-up with listening to a classical pianist) but emphasizes that there's more to Adrian Blair than what happens during the workday.

The key message here is toward the end of the essay after Adrian explains all the different things he does and thinks about during an average day. His concluding question ("Will everything I did today help us get there?") makes the point that while he is busily juggling many tasks, he is not 100 percent sure that everything he is doing is helping the company get from A to Z—or even if Z is the right place to be going. Such reflection is an important

II. A Typical Day

and powerful element of a "typical day" essay. In fact, Adrian could have easily added depth to his account by sharing even more of his introspection. As in other essays in this chapter, maturity and a sense of perspective matter more than the specifics of an average day.

Jay Glaubach

Since graduating from college I have played various roles in various places, including a law student in Boston, a schoolteacher in northern Spain, and an investment banker in New York, London, and Frankfurt. Although it would be impossible to collapse these experiences into a single representative day, I can paint my daily experience with broader strokes. Every day I learned something. Every day I met new people. For these reasons, every day was a challenge.

Every day I learned something new. In Frankfurt I took daily German lessons before work. In New York I learned accounting and corporate valuation on the job. In law school I am learning how to analyze judicial decisions and the policies behind them. Despite the diversity of the past few years, every day has comprised a learning experience.

Every day I interacted with new people from diverse backgrounds. In investment banking I worked with management teams from all over the world, including England, Italy, Finland, and Japan. I argued the merits of the matadors with Spaniards at the bullfights in Madrid. I had dinner with the grandfather of my best friend in Germany, who lived under Hitler's troops in Frankfurt and Khrushchev's in East Berlin. Every day was typified by a unique interaction, however small, with someone who widened my perspective on the world.

Due to these elements, every day has been a challenge. Meeting new people, whether they were clients, coworkers, or classmates, has compelled me to try to understand their distinct viewpoints. Adjusting to new cultural and professional environments has consistently challenged me to readjust my outlook, and staggered me with how much I have yet to learn. My representative day has been alternately frustrating and enrapturing. It has been educational, humbling, enthralling, and demanding. But it has never been boring.

ANALYSIS

This is a wonderful, albeit unconventional essay. Jay is taking a risk here by not describing one single representative day but instead painting a broader picture of how he approaches all days. An essay like this could easily stumble but in this case works beautifully.

Jay has done many things in many cities and wants the admissions committee not to see him as a banker or lawyer but rather as someone who is curious and craves new experiences. Jay is saying to the admissions committee that he will thrive in a diverse place like HBS. Jay's competitive advantage is his breadth of experiences, and the implication that it will contribute to a richer class discussion.

By acknowledging that "every day has been a challenge" and that he is "staggered" by how much he has yet to learn, Jay comes across as humble and approachable. This is critical because if the essay bombs it will be because the tone misses the mark. A key takeaway here is that it is okay to be creative when answering this question. Most people describe a representative day chronologically but as Jay proves, there are other approaches that can work just as well.

LEXIE HALLEN

Early morning. A genomics laboratory in Germany.

I drop reagent into vials containing my skin cell scrapings and the chief scientific officer nods approval. Due diligence is always engaging, but it rarely provides the opportunity to purify one's DNA. I had asked to experiment with the company's new testing kits in order to evaluate whether the technology is simple enough to permit layperson use, as management touts. This analysis will support my investment case.

I next meet with the company's CEO. We trade fresh biotech gossip and then I challenge the growth rates he is projecting for a new business unit, citing evidence from my own industry analysis. In the past few years I have learned to balance a strong company rapport with the ability to ask tough questions. En route to the airport, I call Fidelity portfolio managers with my revised thesis and downgraded numbers on this company and urge them to sell their stock. As the sole European biotechnology analyst, the portfolio managers rely on my guidance to position their funds.

Back in the London office.

I write a note of thanks in Italian to a company that visited our office the previous week. My U.S. counterpart calls. I had suggested that we share industry insights on a regular basis to help each other pick stocks. Now we are working together to determine whether a recent spate of profit warnings from the life science companies are isolated events or indicative of a slowdown in capital equipment spending.

Prowling the corridors, later that day.

Armed with DCF spreadsheets and Play-Doh, I talk through pipeline assumptions with a dubious fund manager. I construct model antibodies and drug receptors to explain how a Nordic company I want him to buy makes drugs with superior side effects. He calls trading to build a position, and I am pleased with the results of my interactive teaching.

Evening, markets closed. Stocks at rest. I wonder what intrigue they will bring tomorrow. I head home to stir-fry a dinner for friends with my new wok.

ANALYSIS

Lexie does a nice job with this essay by demonstrating that she is a hands-on and curious analyst. Throughout the essay Lexie emphasizes that not only can she run the numbers but also ask tough questions of CEOs and then explain complex technologies to fund managers back at the home office. She is engaged in her work but not so deeply so as to lose the necessary perspective to evaluate companies. This maturity is what distinguishes Lexie from the hundreds of other equity analysts who apply to HBS each year. Instead of just saying "this is what I do" Lexie takes it to the next level and demonstrates why she thinks she is more capable than other applicants with similar backgrounds.

The tone of the essay is confident but not condescending and says to HBS: "This is why I am good at what I do—pick me!" You can tell Lexie takes pride in what she does and believes she is helpful to her colleagues. The take-home message here is do not shy away from saying you are good at what you do. However, be careful how you say it. Do not be arrogant; be humble and demonstrate why you are good at your job and why what you do everyday is relevant in a broader context.

BENOIT-OLIVIER BOUREAU

In charge of logistic developments for five Asian factories, I manage project teams for systems implementation and coordinate with local operational teams to make supply chain improvements. I also manage the overall logistics activity of the strategic products manufactured in Asia. These different functions provide an interesting combination of diverse short-term and midterm issues that make no day typical. And today was a representative day.

I started with a phone call to the managers of projects in China and the Philippines. Through these daily reviews I assist them in their difficulties, and we define corrective actions that are followed up the next day.

Mornings are usually kept for operational issues that need to be tackled during the day with Asian teams. Today while shaking hands with the logistics staff of the Bangkok factory, a fault in the invoicing system was reported to me, and I helped to analyze the cause. Later along with the quality department I examined a customer complaint and decided to freeze shipments of a product to check the stock quality.

Lunch was an opportunity to brainstorm with Thailand's production manager on the potential flexibility of a new machine. We planned a meeting to detail the stock savings expected.

Because of the time difference, I usually dedicate afternoons to midterm issues for which I have strong interactions with the French headquarters. Today I consulted with marketing regarding the decision to cease production of a product made in Thailand. Then after a review with the industrial strategy department, I finalized a machine investment midterm plan for the Philippines, in preparation for a business trip there.

My evenings are also active, with dense social life. Today I took a colleague to the opening of my Chinese friend's painting exhibition.

ANALYSIS

The inescapable conclusion from reading Benoit-Olivier's essay is that his days are filled with making decisions and resolving problems across multiple countries and time zones. Without bragging, he conveys the extent and gravity of the responsibility resting on his shoulders. The essay portrays him as a flexible manager, able to make judgment calls on the spot when necessary, but willing to consult matters when more significant repercussions are likely. He comes across as someone able to communicate and work across linguistic and cultural barriers who is respected as a manager for his maturity and extensive experience. All of those aspects make him an attractive candidate and a valuable potential contributor to the diversity at HBS.

If anything, Benoit-Olivier could have improved his conclusion. The very brief references to a social life and his interest in art lack substance a little. Including additional details about these aspects of his life—even if they are not relevant professionally—could have provided further insight into his already well-rounded personality and character.

JASON BOHLE

A Day in the Life

7:30 A.M.: Alarm clock blares with the Beatles: "Wake up. Get out of bed. Drag a comb across my head. Catch the bus in seconds flat." Perform said lyrics.

8 A.M.: Catch train, skim the headlines of the *WSJ* and then delve into the international section. Get so absorbed almost miss my stop.

9 A.M.–12 P.M.: Review cash flow and valuation analyses prepared by members of the Latin American team. Work with team to confirm growth assumptions and discuss sensitivity of investor returns to currency assumptions.

1 P.M.: Call investment bankers or officers of an investment target and ask questions about inconsistencies or confusing aspects of the financial models they provided. Ask for updates on previously requested questions or documents.

2 P.M.: For a different deal, field a curve ball thrown by the target company's lawyers. Work with these lawyers and our counsel to analyze and discuss the effects of proposed changes in the legal and tax structure of the transaction.

3 P.M.: Call CEO and CFO of target company to tell them what progress we have made and what we still need from their bankers or management team. Brainstorm with them on solutions to comments made by the lawyers. Outline steps for the next few days.

4 P.M.: Meet with my supervisor and the Latin American team. Update them on my progress and highlight any key outstanding issues or pressure points that must be resolved.

4:30 P.M.: Begin gathering and processing information that will be presented to our investment committee in a few weeks.

6:30 P.M.: Plan goals that need to be accomplished for tomorrow's ten-day trip to Mexico and Brazil.

7 P.M.: Start home. Read.

8 P.M.: Run five miles, watching sunset along the Hudson River.

9:30 P.M.: Meet friends for dinner, jazz show or a movie.

ANALYSIS

This is a straightforward, solid essay that does not try to blow you away with superhuman feats, but rather establishes Jason as a hard worker who manages to maintain a reasonably balanced life despite being in a high-stress, fast-paced industry. The best line in the essay—and the one that makes you think Jason is probably a pretty good guy—is the first one about performing the Beatles lyrics. It is a good (and funny) opening and sets a relaxed tone for the rest of the essay. Everything that follows is a fairly standard description of a day in the life of a banker. Nonetheless, Jason's incorporation of a consistent set of references to Latin America and international affairs helps him stand out a little from the group of his investment banking peers.

While overall this essay does a good job describing a typical day, Jason could have added a little more depth to it. He could have peppered his day with stronger instances of taking a leadership role or simply added more introspective details. However, you do not have to hit a grand slam with all six or seven essays to make a good impression. In fact, forcing six or seven supposedly world-beating essays out of thin air will probably help you a lot less than just answering some of the questions simply and matter-of-factly. That is what Jason has done here and it worked well for him.

III. DEFINING MOMENT

We all experience "defining moments;" significant events that can have a major impact on our lives. Briefly describe such an event and how it has affected you.

Before starting to write, it is worth taking a moment to think about what this question is really asking, as well as what it is not. A number of applicants make the mistake of equating *defining* with something heroic or noble and try to describe a moment that fits accordingly. Try not to fall into this trap. Do not try to convince the admissions committee that your defining moment is more spectacular than those of your peers; instead, simply show how one moment or experience has had a significant impact on your development as an individual.

Some defining moments are in fact heroic (like learning to overcome a disability); if you have such a moment to share—great! Just make sure to be humble about what happened. On the other hand, do not worry if what you have to offer seems mundane; the specifics of the moment matter a lot less than what you learned from it.

This is your opportunity to tell a story about how you became you. Be brave. Be funny. Be introspective. Be all those things if you can, but definitely be honest about how what happened changed who you are. What should you avoid? Being shy. Reserved writing usually is not good writing, and it certainly will not tell anyone anything profoundly interesting about you. The point: take a chance with the story you choose to tell.

—Valerie Valtz

VINCENT CHEUNG

Earlier this year, I returned to the place I once left as a child: Asia. During my six-month transfer to Bain & Company's offices in the region, I traveled through some of the world's most impressive airports and tallest skyscrapers. I also witnessed firsthand the poverty that plagued neighborhoods across Asia, from the countryside of Vietnam to street corners near my grandmother's home in Manila. Once, on a trip to Jakarta, my taxi was caught in traffic. As I looked out from my window, I saw a boy, no more than five years old, slowly strolling through lanes on the highway with bags of peanuts. He knocked on every window along the way trying to make a sale, but was ignored by passengers sitting comfortably inside Mercedes sedans chatting on cellular phones.

The prevalent and pedestrian nature of this scene made it a "defining moment" for me. In fact, the lessons from my transfer have inspired my long-term goal to close the widening gap between Asia's elite and its poor. During an e-commerce strategy project for a software client in greater China, I saw a vibrant, entrepreneurial community eager to discover how the new economy will redefine Asia. I am convinced that technology will bring unprecedented opportunities for those enchained by the status quo to lift themselves up. I also experienced the intricacies in dealings with government bureaucracy in my work with a British consumer-product client frustrated with its state-owned monopoly partner in Vietnam. I hope to apply my private sector experience to help development agencies such as the Asia Development Bank confront similar challenges and reach those truly in need.

As Asia continues to bridge its economic divide, the future depends on a new generation of business leaders who embrace innovation and understand how to bring about transformation to a region at the crossroads of change. I am committed to be a part of this *next big wave*.

ANALYSIS

Vincent's defining moment is in some ways unremarkable. He is stuck in traffic in the back of a taxi. The only thing that is exotic is the location: Jakarta. After spending weeks jetting around the region from gleaming office tower to gleaming office tower, Vincent stares out the window of the taxi and sees a boy trying to make a few cents selling peanuts. It is a sad but common sight in Southeast Asia, but gets Vincent thinking that he has to do something to make the situation better. Vincent's decision is to dedicate his career to helping those in need. It is a noble goal and one Vincent seems determined to pursue. This is a good example of an essay that shows that an ordinary experience (sitting in a taxi in traffic) can be every bit as transforming as something spectacular. Remember: it is what you learn from what happened, not what happened, that is important.

While this ending successfully navigates Vincent's journey from Asia to present day, its conclusion is a little open-ended. After giving specific examples as to how the defining moment has impacted him, Vincent takes us back to fifty-thousand feet and vaguely refers to being part of "the next big wave." A more tangible ending would make his story even more compelling.

Amanda Morris

In the summer of 1995, I was selected to serve as an exchange officer with the British Royal Navy. Thus far, my experiences in the U.S. Navy had been interesting, exciting, and amazingly fun: flying in helicopters, firing machine guns, diving to twelve thousand feet in a submarine, etc. I was now assigned to a British destroyer in the North Atlantic, participating in the most intensive assessment program known to the Royal Navy. It included onboard facilitators simulating the most realistic, warlike conditions.

When "war" broke out, explosions went off, power went out, passageways filled with smoke, and casualties lay screaming. I was a firefighter on the damage control team, dispatched to fight a fire in the engine room. I watched three of my men leap down a hatch, and then heard a facilitator yell, "In ten seconds, that fire will spread to the entire ship! What are you going to do?" After a gut-wrenching pause, I ran to the hatch, closed it, and tightened it down.

I forced myself to remember that this was only a drill. It was a defining moment. I had just made a decision that cost the lives of three men. In reality, would I have been able to justify my actions, knowing I had done the right thing and served the greater good? Could I have looked the families of those men in the eye and told them that I had no choice? This event illustrated to me that the greatest challenge of leadership is making impossibly tough decisions when a decision must be made. I learned that after all the soul-searching, you must stand by your decision and move on. I also now see what is meant when people refer to the loneliness of command, the loneliness of leadership.

ANALYSIS

Once the "explosions" have stopped and the "casualties" have been removed, we are left with a young officer who has learned in a simulated environment valuable real-world lessons about the difficulties of leadership. Amanda clearly demonstrates strong leadership skills but also an impressive level of maturity by writing about the challenges associated with being a leader. This is a good example of a writer who has taken the time to think deeply about what she has learned from an experience (in this case, that being a leader is not always all it is cracked up to be). When writing your own essay you should take the time to think about not only the obvious lessons but also what you did not expect to learn.

Regardless of the substance of the lesson you draw from your defining moment, however, try to explain how it has impacted your life in a broader sense. This is the one thing arguably missing from Amanda's esay. Although she pinpoints how she arrived at a deeper understanding of leadership, she does not tell us anything about how the experience influenced her subsequent choices or decisions.

Constantine Dimizas

Upon graduating from college, everyone expected me to join my father's business because I had been working for him part-time since the age of twelve. However, a year before graduation, the firm started experiencing financial difficulties that could have led to bankruptcy. By living through my father's agony to save his business, I experienced firsthand the difficulties and uncertainties involved in his line of work. In addition, the bleak outlook for most small businesses made my future seem even more uncertain had I decided to enter this field.

I faced a dilemma: whether to join the family business or pursue my passion for finance, which was my field of study and a promising sector in Greece at the time. To everyone's surprise, I decided to seek employment in the financial sector. After numerous interviews and several offers, I followed my mentor's advice (my professor Lila Mordochae) and one week after graduating from college I was hired as a financial analyst at Telesis Investment Bank.

In retrospect, the crisis in my father's business has had a lasting impact on my life. This experience taught me to think and plan strategically, with the security and well-being of my family in mind. Experiencing the effects of this crisis, I recognized the significance of thoroughly evaluating the repercussions of my decisions on others prior to any action. In addition, I learned the value of being united with others at all times—family, friends or colleagues—especially during difficult times.

I also realized the significance of being financially independent and of assuming full responsibility for my future. Even though my parents had instilled in me the importance of saving money for a rainy day, it was through this experience that I realized how important it is to do so. I have learned to lead a balanced life: living within my means, enjoying the fruits of my labor, but also saving for future and unexpected needs.

ANALYSIS

Constantine uses his decision not to join his father's firm as a way to explain how he came to prioritize what is important to him. Watching his father's company teeter on the brink of bankruptcy and then deciding not to help him had to be a tremendously difficult decision. It is a decision that is easy not to like. At the same time, though, it is inspiring because Constantine is doing what he thinks is right in terms of his long-term priorities.

The essay successfully outlines many important lessons that Constantine learned while making this career decision. It would have been even more powerful if he had elaborated on some of the details of his thought process. Nonetheless, as a reader, you finish the essay thinking that Constantine is someone who knows very clearly what he wants from life.

The lesson to keep in mind while writing your own essay: have a point of view and communicate it clearly. It is more important to express what is important than to tell a beautiful story that does not say much about what you believe or who you are.

BRAD FINKBEINER

I didn't know what to believe, and with hypothermia setting in, I didn't know if I could make it. The water was 48°F and I had been in it for thirty minutes. Luckily, I was headed back to shore, but it had been a frustrating experience. I had always been a good swimmer and I could have made it back before now, but those weren't the rules. The twelve of us were instructed to swim and finish as a team. Then again, the same people told us the water would be warm and to jump in without wetsuits. After another twenty minutes and constant encouragement, we finally made it. My feeling of pride and newfound confidence showed me just how much I had needed the challenge.

Eagle Lake Wilderness Camp in the Colorado Rockies provided fourteen days of cold, hunger, and exhaustion, which turned into a lifetime of opportunities. Growing up, I was smart and perceptive, but also reserved. I needed to break that paradigm. I needed confidence in my ability to handle stressful, unpredictable situations so that I could develop my potential as a leader.

Our swim was only one of ten challenges faced by our team. I learned much more than how to survive hypothermia, navigate a free rappel, live off the wilderness, and complete a high-altitude half-marathon. I revealed some of my natural leadership qualities like self-understanding and sustained motivation. I demonstrated how to work effectively within teams. I acquired the confidence to pursue leadership responsibilities. I found the will to pursue difficult and exhausting goals along with the stamina to accomplish them.

And I learned how to be most effective by encouraging and developing others.

Our team mantra, "This wasn't in the brochure," has since reflected the excitement and challenge of my life. Without the lessons and confidence gained from this experience, I would never have had the ability to run student governments, organize community initiatives or lead consulting project teams.

ANALYSIS

The outdoors-experience-that-changed-my-life story runs the risk of sounding all too familiar but does not in this case, thanks to Brad's nice sense of storytelling. Brad goes into the experience as a shy kid without a lot of confidence but emerges from the hypothermia, the half-marathon, and the free rappel as a more courageous and confident person. The transformation is striking and Brad proves that he is someone open to new experiences. Brad does a nice job with this essay by describing in detail both how he changed and what he learned from the experiences. When writing you own essay, if you are worried your topic might not come across as super-original take the time to tell a compelling narrative with lots of colorful details. The more specific you are, the better your essay will be.

Brad concludes his essay by mentioning his participation in student government, community work, and leadership at work. These are great illustrations of the impact of his "defining moment." Given the word-count constraints, there is no room left in this essay to discuss them. However, they are very good themes to pick up his other essays. If used well, such common threads can make the complete set coherent and mutually supporting.

ANONYMOUS

The most defining moment that I have experienced is overcoming my handicap by learning to walk.

At the age of one, I had to undergo surgery to my spine due to a nonmalignant tumor. The tumor was removed successfully, but during the surgery my nerves were damaged, which resulted in paraplegia. Several doctors told my parents that I would never be able to walk and I was placed in a school for the handicapped.

I was a happy child and at school I ranked the highest in class. As I was growing up, however, I came to have a number of exciting friends, who were able to walk. This made it harder for me to be limited in my own movement. Fortunately, it stimulated my mother to approach a well-known surgeon, who made it possible for me to walk with braces on my legs. After three years I became restless again and I longed to go to a normal school. I was the first in the special school's history to "escape." But my most challenging accomplishment was yet to come. I refused to have any doctor draw my boundaries and I pushed myself through several more operations and an intense period of physical therapy. The impossible came true, as I became able to walk with crutches.

Any handicap will generate a significant amount of emotional turmoil in a person's life. Although I still walk with the help of crutches, my disability hasn't created any barriers in my life that I could not resolve. The contrary happened, as conquering my handicap offered me a sense of achievement and self-confidence that enables me to confront the challenges of life audaciously and with a positive mind. Achieving an accomplishment that I could initially only dream of had a huge influence on my personality.

ANALYSIS

From the opening line, the author's matter-of-fact voice reveals the enormity of the handicap he has overcome. The essay touches us but does not ask for our sympathy. Instead, we are given the impression of an individual grateful for everything he has and eager to embrace life.

There is no question this essay is "heroic"—where it shines, though, is its tone. It is warm, touching, and inspirational without being preachy. While walking with crutches for the first time is an amazing moment in its own right, what will resonate most with the reader is what kind of person the author is. The lesson: it does not matter if your story is heroic or humble but you had better come across as someone worth getting to know.

Larry Wasserman

I've never been much of an athlete. I love participating in sports and I enjoy competition, but asking me to do anything besides running in a straight line has never yielded stellar results. For this reason, I was a sprinter on my high school's track team. In my junior year, the coach asked for volunteers for the pole vault, specifically sprinters who were relatively compact in stature and light in weight. This described me perfectly, and I did not have enough muscle for the shot put (or the javelin, or the discus, or the hammer throw), so I figured I would give it a try.

After practicing for a month, I had scrapes all over my legs from falling on the ground. I had knocked the wind out of myself on several occasions when the pole rebounded into my chest, and, in one nearly successful attempt, had hit my head on the bar right before I fell back to earth (and by earth, I mean the hard, rocky ground). My near misses, I was told, were because I was hesitant; I was letting fear of failing and falling get the best of me. I needed to just go for it, to forget about the potential pain, and trust myself. I kept practicing.

I remember the day I actually made it over the bar. I took ten quick measured steps, pole in hand. On the eleventh, I slowly lowered the pole toward the ground. On the twelfth, I jammed it into the ground, pushing as hard as I could, and rode the pole into the air. I landed on the mat on the other side of the bar, which did not come tumbling down upon me. I stared up at the sky, dazed and amazed, and realized for the first time that the biggest boundaries I faced in my life would come from my own fears. As long as I persisted and kept a sense of humor about things that didn't necessarily come easily to me, I could never be disappointed with myself, and I'd be surprised by what I could accomplish.

ANALYSIS

Larry's essay is funny, upbeat, and delightfully self-aware. He is determined to overcome his lack of natural athletic ability and is willing to put up with a lot of pain and frustration to accomplish something that initially seems completely unattainable. Larry shows he is responsive to criticism, a sign of maturity, and toward the end of the essay revels in his realization that fear is the only thing that can hold him back in life. Larry does everything he can to make his essay memorable. Pole-vaulting is unusual enough to stand out, the essay's writing style is fluid and engaging, and Larry uses the conclusion to explain how this defining moment has impacted his view on life. The story is an impressive transformation and a good example of an essay that says a lot in only three hundred words.

ANONYMOUS

I picked up the telephone one Wednesday this April and immediately knew something was wrong from the tone of my second brother's voice. My youngest brother had tried to take his life. He lay in the hospital but didn't want our parents to find out. He had been clinically depressed for some time, but had said nothing to any of us. His words, his actions, and the results of the tests administered all indicated that he would probably try again.

That call shocked me. The following months have changed my approach to life.

I found the ensuing two weeks emotionally and physically draining. I spent sleepless nights deciding whether to tell my parents. I also struggled to reconcile the fact that my actions have not always reflected my personal priorities. My mind dwelt on the number of times I had put work before a call to my brothers, or a visit to my parents in West Yorkshire. The event made me acutely aware of the trade-offs I have made and continue to make. At the moment my family needs my support, yet at the same time work is entering a critical phase. I therefore spend less time with friends. I am aware of the need to constantly reassess what my priorities are.

I also found it very difficult to accept that I had missed the signs of my brother's depression. I thought I understood him because we share the same family and have had similar experiences. If I could miss something like this with my own brother, with whom I have a familial bond, how can I ever be sure of my impact on those who I know less well? I now think more deeply about all my relationships, both personal and work, and consider how my words and actions will be understood from their perspective.

ANALYSIS

This essay does not try to paint the author in a positive light, nor does it tell a tale of how the author overcame some great obstacle. Its honesty, though, speaks volumes. We feel the author's pain when he writes that he missed signs of his brother's depression and we struggle with him as he tries to figure out what really matters in life. If the actual moment is not something we can relate to, the ensuing emotions are.

For obvious reasons, this is a powerful essay. We chose it because it is an excellent example of an author taking a huge risk by revealing something personal. It is an interesting example, too, because it does not try to neatly tie up loose ends or finish on an uplifting note, as most other essays do. Nonetheless, the impact of the events on the author's personality is clear, and he comes across as mature, and, owing to this experience, exceptionally self-aware.

ANONYMOUS

The 747 banked sharply to its left, its wing seemingly inches from clipping an apartment complex. I was on my way home to Hong Kong from a holiday in Taiwan. Six months earlier, in July 1997, the approach to Kai Tak had terrified me. Landing at Kai Tak was, even for a veteran flier, harrowing; pilots had to dodge buildings, turn at the last possible moment and then land on a narrow runway jutting into the harbor.

That first flight scared me, though, not just because I was unfamiliar with the steep turn but also because I was, quite literally, flying into the unknown. I was moving to Hong Kong from Washington, D.C. where I had lived for five years. I did not have a job, I did not speak Cantonese, and I knew (barely) one person, a family friend who had said I could house-sit for a month while he was in the U.S. I would like to think I arrived in Hong Kong craving adventure but the truth is I was apprehensive and not sure I could pull it off.

Fast-forward six months to that flight from Taipei: as the plane landed I thought, "Wow, I'm home." That idea (that Hong Kong could be "home") surprised me but also made me realize how much I had grown in those six months. I had sweated through a steamy Hong Kong summer; I had turned my one contact into a network of acquaintances; I had used that network to find a job as a reporter for *Time* magazine; and, perhaps most important, I had proven I could survive—no, thrive—in a city vastly different from those I had known in the States. I was proud of myself, but not just because I had learned to live in Hong Kong. I was proud because I was confident and curious and eager to gobble up everything Hong Kong had in store for me.

ANALYSIS

This essay is a wonderfully crafted story of personal growth. The two jumbo-jet landings spaced six months apart provide an excellent parallel structure for creating a contrast. At first glance, the essay might appear as a simple anecdote about getting used to landing at Kai Tak or living in Hong Kong. But that would be just a cursory interpretation. The author uses the text to convey his willingness to take risks and ability to persevere when faced with a seemingly overwhelming challenge. His professional successes—and his ability to call Hong Kong "home"—speak volumes about his initiative and ability to adapt to a new environment. After reading the concluding words, we imagine the author to be a very resilient individual, hungry to experience new environments and completely unwilling to rest on the laurels of comfort and familiarity.

The author takes an interesting liberty with the concept of the "defining moment." Rather than focus on a specific instant, he uses the plane's landing as a point of departure for his exploration of six months of learning and personal development. While somewhat unorthodox, the approach works quite well.

IV. EXPERIENCING A SETBACK OR A FAILURE

Describe a setback, disappointment, or occasion of failure that you have experienced. How did you manage the situation, and what did you learn from it?

Life would be dull if you got everything you wanted without having to struggle a bit. This question is all about how you deal with adversity. The key here is to turn whatever setback you experienced into something positive. Do not dwell on the disappointment—although describe it vividly—but rather focus on how you solved the problem and what you learned.

The following essays are terrific examples of individuals who did just that—they demonstrated initiative, adaptability, self-awareness, and strength of character in their reactions. These are stories both big and small. In choosing your own example, do not fret about finding a grand tale; this essay is about perceptiveness and introspection on your part, regardless of the scale of the event. You do not have to paint yourself as a phoenix rising dramatically from the ashes.

The failure essay is not trying to pick holes in your character; on the contrary, it is trying to build it up. Simply structured, it should step through the context, the setback, the consequences, the lessons, the solution, and the future application of your key takeaways.

We all have been beaten to the canvas, we have been dumped, we have flunked a test . . . and we should be thankful for it all. To fail is to have tried. The courage is in the ability to learn from your mistakes. This essay is your opportunity to show how you stepped back in the ring, found somebody new and aced the test. In the words of the great British leader, Sir Winston Churchill, "Difficulties mastered are opportunities won." Show you believe that.

—Jamyn Edis

CHRIS WITHERS

A scaffold bolt had just whistled past my ear. It was my third day on a construction site and I had been assigned six men to complete the foundations. I was only twenty years old and lacked experience and confidence, which the men were exploiting. By the end of the week, another engineer had replaced me.

My first reaction was relief, but that was soon replaced by boredom with my new filing duties. I realized that my lack of training and experience had meant that I wasn't ready to manage a team. I met with the site manager and asked to shadow another engineer for the next two weeks to learn how to lead on a construction site.

I quickly learned the basic technical aspects of the role, but, more importantly, I recognized that the other engineers had a directive style, in contrast to my desire to lead by consensus. My problems had been largely caused by my leadership style, which had not been appropriate for the situation and which I had not adjusted appropriately.

After two weeks, I persuaded the site manager to give me another team. At the start of this role I adopted an authoritative manner, which was similar to that expected by the team of laborers. Once I had developed a working relationship of mutual respect with the team, I was able to relax some aspects of the direct management approach and build a rapport with the men.

This experience allowed me to practice different leadership styles and to understand the need to adapt my approach to suit the situation, the individual, and the team. I also learned about the role of confidence and credibility when leading a team, as well as the importance of training and mentoring for new starters.

ANALYSIS

In recounting the story of a setback in the workplace, Chris delivers a well-crafted narrative with pertinent lessons. With the detail of a bolt whistling past his head, the story kicks off with a punchy opener, providing both dynamism and humor. By the end of the first paragraph we know the context and also the setback Chris faces.

The story moves on quickly and Chris crisply frames a solution—the all-important element of a failure essay. He then drills deeper into the progress he makes, illustrating changed behaviors and maturity. What makes him stand out is his self-awareness, his ability to move swiftly, providing insight into his adaptive character. A smart move here is to tie in the evolution of his leadership style, which should be an important theme in all HBS essays.

This is a very strong essay. It is tightly structured, stylized, and presents lessons within an appropriate storyline. Chris might have improved it slightly by removing some of the redundancy in the final two paragraphs and using the extra space to include concrete examples of how he applied the lessons outside the building site—whether in other work environments or in his personal life.

EUGENIA GIBBONS

My first project at Accenture consisted of an SAP implementation for Chile's largest copper mining company. Thanks to the experience I had acquired on the human resources module, I was asked to train the geographical divisions' personnel. I had spent several days preparing the training material and rehearsing, when I arrived to the Chuquicamata site, the largest open sky mine in the world, where forty administrative staff and supervisors were expecting me for weeklong training. They were all men and most of them former miners. The first session was terrible! I did not get any attention from my audience, and they were even disrespectful toward me.

There is a strong cultural rivalry between Chile and Argentina, to the point that some Chilean clients refuse to be served by Argentinean consulting teams. Additionally, very few women work in Chile, and even fewer are executives. That day, I had the feeling I was paying for both being an Argentinean and a woman. However, I was extremely disappointed with my own performance and incapacity to control the group.

Toward the late afternoon, I interrupted the formal session and opened up the dialogue, reinforcing why I thought this training was important for all participants, and how it would affect their daily work. I also clearly stated how unprofessional their attitude had been and how it made me feel. After discussing what they wanted to get out of the training, we agreed on having eight extra hours to compensate for the time lost. From that moment on the group's attitude changed radically, my role was accepted and the training turned out to be a great success.

What I learned from this episode was above all the absolute imperative to adapt the message and format of any presentation to its audience, and to identify and address the potential sources of conflict up front.

ANALYSIS

Eugenia finds herself in a tough spot. Many professionals will have encountered a similar situation—on unfamiliar ground, feeling under-qualified and facing a hostile client. Eugenia provides a great deal of detail in her story and this helps the reader empathize with her situation as a woman facing cultural and sexist obstacles. With a limited word count you do not want to over-invest in setting the stage, but at the same time it is critical to take the time to tell a story people can relate to.

In describing her next steps, Eugenia walks through a three-point action plan and then assesses how she improved the situation. As in most good failure essays, the concluding outcome is positive. Eugenia demonstrates that she is able to react to setbacks in a mature and rational fashion, no matter how stressful the situation.

JOHN RICHARD

One of my greatest struggles has been with my speech. I had a stuttering problem from age four that was a constant source of self-doubt until recently. In fourth grade, my parents took me to a speech pathologist in Houston who, through a yearlong program, "cured" my stuttering. After Exxon hired me in 1997, I experienced a demoralizing failure of speech that made me realize my stuttering was definitely not cured.

The cost engineering section had gathered to update our new worldwide manager on current projects and initiatives. We were supposed to introduce ourselves and summarize our activities. When it came time for my introduction, I turned toward him, reached out my hand in greeting and said, "I'm J . . ." As I tried to say my name, my vocal cords locked. For what seemed like an eternity, I tried to force my way past the block, but the embarrassed stares from my peers and supervisors just increased my paralysis. Eventually, I made it through the introduction and work summary but not before having that experience burned in my memory. Immediately after that incident, I started searching for a "miracle" drug to cure stuttering. After a few frustrating months, I realized that no cure existed so I purchased a self-help book. I practiced the exercises for several months and noticed some improvement in my speech, but when disfluencies still occurred, I felt helpless. After two more years of avoiding difficult speaking situations, I consulted the Stuttering Foundation of America, which made me understand that stuttering is something that can never be completely cured but can be managed through self-awareness. To gain awareness of my stuttering, I have been keeping a daily journal of my speech habits. I document how my speech muscles react in stuttering situations and practice modifying or relaxing those muscles in similar situations. My newfound control over my speech has led me to actively seek out speaking situations that I avoided before. For instance, I was elected president of my homeowners' association, and I have shared several safety learnings in front of the sixty employees in my department. As my success grows, so, too, does my confidence to where I rarely experience speech blocks like I did in 1997. However, I've realized that I must practice, practice, practice and that I will be doing this the rest of my life.

While the concept of practice makes perfect isn't new, it has taken on new meaning for how I lead my life. I know that every aspect of my life where I'd like to see improvement must involve a substantial amount of practice, from negotiating skills to surfing, from networking with colleagues to training my dog.

ANALYSIS

John is brave to share a great personal challenge and his journey to conquer it. After a brief exposition of his stuttering problem, John dives right into the excruciating moment when he was confronted with an obstacle he thought he had overcome years ago. As a reader you empathize with him and want him to succeed. This essay, though, is not a tearjerker, and when writing your own essay you should be careful not to tell a sad story just to earn cheap points (because you will not). We feel his burning embarrassment, but we do not pity him.

John demonstrates his resolve by trying a self-help plan and seeking outside counsel. He then goes on to give real examples of

IV. Experiencing a Setback or a Failure

how he applied these lessons and came to the realization that nothing will be solved without practice and hard work. And although this lesson may seem superficial at first, it captures the essence of a good failure essay—namely, finding the inner strength to surmount an obstacle no matter how daunting.

Jordan Burton

In the course of only a few months, my Bain colleague Graham and I transformed ChangeAddress.com from an idea into a company. We raised $1.8 million in venture funding led by multibillion-dollar Cox Enterprises, brought together a powerful and motivated board (including a former postmaster general and chief of staff under Lyndon Johnson) and hired nineteen incredibly talented individuals. We built the most feature-rich and user-friendly online address change service available to the forty-four million annual U.S. movers.

By the late fall of 2000, revenues were growing nearly 50 percent month-to-month. This was not, however, sufficient to cover our cash burn rate. Though we had allocated resources with significant conservatism, we had always known that we would need an additional round of approximately $5 million to generate positive operating cash flows. In a series of frustrating setbacks, several strategic and venture capital investors pulled back their once overwhelming interest, leaving us with dissolution as our only option.

Despite our profound feelings of loss, Graham and I approached the wind-down with the same degree of professionalism and courage as our initial fund-raising. We identified every stakeholder involved in our business, and made a joint decision that the welfare of our employees would come first and our personal financial considerations would come last. We leveraged our network of Atlanta business contacts to help each of our workers find jobs and arranged to sell the assets of the company to our business partner,

Moving.com, for enough money to avoid bankruptcy and return some money to our preferred shareholders.

Despite the financial failure, the learning experience from ChangeAddress.com transcends the dollars and cents—Graham and I learned how to inspire a group of individuals to follow a vision and create something out of nothing. And we learned that, despite the risks and uncertainties we face, the only true mistake is to be afraid to make one.

ANALYSIS

Jordan's story is a terrific illustration of what makes a successful failure essay. It demonstrates his individual drive, adaptability, and personal integrity. Furthermore, these characteristics are framed within a compelling narrative, striking a balance between its depth and being to the point. The text is tightly constructed with a beginning, middle, and end—a fundamental structural element of storytelling.

From the get-go, Jordan presents a scene that will be recognizable to many pre-MBA students. Jordan does not come across as a young hothead, expecting undeserved reward, but rather elicits sympathy as someone who cares deeply about the people who work for him and deeply regrets having let them down. Jordan is cognizant that his setback affects a great many constituents. Furthermore, he is concerned about his fiduciary duty to the stakeholders, placing himself at the end of the line for financial compensation. This shows tremendous maturity and leaves the reader with a sense that these characteristics will stick with Jordan throughout his career.

CRAIG ELLIS

Time never passes more slowly than when waiting for an actor to remember his next line. During my senior year in high school I earned the opportunity to direct a play from casting to curtain call. However, what should have been a pleasant, two-and-a-half-hour performance turned into a four-hour ordeal. I honestly felt sorry for the audience.

I did not realize the problems my casting had caused until two weeks before the show when the lead actress was suspended and the lead actor was still using cue cards he had hidden around the set. I should have mitigated my poor evaluation of my cast by replacing the lead actress and adapting my directing style to reap the talent of my lead actor. Instead, I continued with my plan, confident that my two actors would pull themselves together. The lead actress assured me she would be ready for the show, and the lead actor, who later went to Juilliard, would surely perform to his skill level.

My confidence was shattered that first long performance. My mistake was in my casting, but my failure was in my unwillingness to make the changes the play needed to succeed. This experience strengthened my skills in critically evaluating the strengths of my team members, but the lesson that has haunted me is that it is never too late to change direction when success demands it.

Years later, when I re-created the process monitoring system at the Koch refinery, the first version was complete when I realized that major revisions were needed to keep the system running after I was gone; I had to change direction. I spent two months working extra hours to complete the revisions. Six months later, my assistance has not once been needed to maintain or operate the system.

ANALYSIS

You can almost feel Craig squirming in his seat as his actors bungle yet another line. But in this essay the writer does not miss a trick, delivering an offbeat example of personal disappointment. This essay is a good example that you do not have to tell a story related to your job. In fact, lots of people do not. Do, though, remember to tie what you learned back to why you want to go to business school.

Here, Craig is conscious to telegraph his key takeaways through a series of "shoulda, woulda, coulda" moments, showing how he wished he could have acted differently. This addresses the topic's requirement for personal learning, and makes the reader believe that the protagonist really did assimilate these lessons. In addition, the essay neatly dovetails into a second example, which illustrates the application of lessons learned to his project at the Koch refinery. This symmetry between the creative and commercial strands of the essay shows Craig as a well-rounded individual.

Irfhan Rawji

We had one thousand children and one hundred counselors on a cruise ship bound to Alaska. The project was the Young Presidents Organization family cruise, and I was contracted to help coordinate the youth activities under difficult constraints—space, time, and resources being the greatest of these.

To provide our clients with a memorable experience, we built a system that was capable of manipulating thousands of variables (staff, space, time, budget) into a solution that would allow each child maximum exposure to his or her favorite activity.

This solution was so complex that it confused the parents, children, and our staff alike. Extreme dissatisfaction emanated only three hours into our 168-hour contract. The project lead looked to me to uncover the source of our problem, as well as provide and implement the appropriate solution.

By hour twelve we had regrouped and redrawn our approach with a new understanding. Our objective was to ensure that each child went to bed with a smile; it was not to provide a custom adventure. Children were less worried about what they were doing, than who they were with—fun, motivated counselors in an environment that included friends. We achieved tremendous success, resulting in accolades not only for our service delivery, but also for our flexibility and quick turnaround.

I learned that it is important to fully understand the client and her/his end objectives. Additionally, it is important to deliver a solution that is complex enough to meet those needs—but no more. We had spent too much time engineering the solution, and not enough understanding the problem. What seemed like a new and innovative approach was just a complicated, difficult, and time-consuming method of delivering fun.

ANALYSIS

Irfhan's essay is a good story about admitting a mistake and being willing to throw out lots of hard work and start over at a moment's notice. Irfhan fails to untangle the Gordian knot of his situation, but rather than admitting defeat, cuts through the problem with a simple approach. This shows creativity on his part as well as a lack of stubbornness. The result is that even though his initial plan did not work as he had hoped, he was able to save the day and prevent the cruise from being a total disaster.

The story is well-paced, delivering its central message within a structured framework: situation, complication, solution, take-aways. While you should feel free to experiment with the form your essay takes, with a limited word count you may not want to stray too far from this basic structure. One caveat: ending on a negative note can leave the reader with the impression that the failure was total and irreparable. In Irfhan's experience, this was not the case and the final paragraph does illustrate the lessons learned. Nonetheless, unless you have a good reason not to do so, it is generally best to conclude with a positive accent.

THOMSON NGUY

I had just arrived in my unit, fresh from the U.S. Army Ranger School and the officer basic course, when my company set out on a twelve-mile foot march. By mile five, my radioman fell out of formation, unable to carry the extra weight of the radio along with the normal seventy pounds. Anxious to make a good impression, I eagerly took on his burden.

Around mile eight, I myself started running out of breath. I refused Sergeant Nelson's offer of help, determined to conquer this obstacle with tenacity, determination, and the stubborn refusal to give up. I marched for another two miles, hyperventilating each step of the way. Then, to my supreme embarrassment, I passed out. The platoon sauntered by me, their stricken platoon leader, as I lay along the side of the road while my sergeants doused canteen water on my groggy head.

I failed because of my pride. It was a lesson that would lead to a fundamental shift in my understanding of leadership. Instead of trying to be the hero of my platoon, I soon learned to accept the help of my sergeants. The ultimate success of the platoon depended on the actions of my squad and team leaders. The reserve of talent and potential there were far greater than anything I could have accomplished on my own. The best leaders, I learned, subsume their need for individual recognition in order to let their subordinates and superiors shine.

I changed my approach and our platoon excelled. Two months later, the battalion embarked on a twenty-five-mile foot march, a test of character and will. I marched at the head of the platoon, setting the example and encouraging the soldiers. My squad and team leaders kept their men in line, distributing the heavy equipment among themselves. Of the twenty-seven platoons in the battalion, ours was the only one of two that finished without a soldier falling out. As for the radio, between myself, the radioman, Sergeant Nelson, Sergeant Gryder, and Sergeant Brown, we all shared the burden.

ANALYSIS

"Rangers lead the way!" is the motto of the U.S. Army Rangers. In this essay, Thomson demonstrates how he took this philosophy to an extreme, and as a consequence, failed those under his command. This story is great in highlighting the danger of hubris, and overcoming obstacles with energy, grit, and determination. It leaves the reader rooting for a successful outcome after a humiliating initial setback.

Fortunately for Thomson, he does not fall into the trap of assuming his idiosyncratic setting is enough to carry the essay. Instead, he shows an appreciation of learning through bitter experience. In this regard, he shows the applicability of a lesson across a spectrum of situations. As with the other successful failure essays, this story is dynamic, structured, and compelling, illustrating the evolution of an individual and a leader.

Anonymous

During my first consulting project, I was asked to construct a sales plan for an insurance company. The first step was to meet Adam, the director of sales, to discuss forecasting assumptions. A list of questions in hand, I knocked on the door. To my surprise, Adam was very formal in his reception. He did not understand why we were meeting, so I explained that I would be creating sales plans. At that point, he became outright hostile. He barked out his nonanswers to my questions and informed me he was very busy . . . preparing sales plans. Before I could suggest cooperation, I was ushered out, and the door slammed behind me. Too shocked to react to the secretary's condescending smirk, I attempted to grasp why a textbook opportunity for teamwork became such a spectacular failure. What had I done to attract such hostility? I had just wanted to help. I called my engagement manager to complain, but he just accused me of handling the situation poorly. I was crushed and convinced that I was not cut out for consulting.

To this day, I am not sure why Adam was so hostile. Retrospectively, I can only guess that he was insulted and threatened, because no one had formally requested his assistance. Instead, a twenty-two-year-old appeared in his office, ready to perform one of his most challenging tasks.

Adam and I never became friends, but the incident profoundly affected the way I communicate. Now, every time I interview a client, I begin by exploring and allaying any fears the person might have. I explain the project's rationale and seek a frank reaction. The rapport thus established makes the interviewees comfortable enough to share private opinions. This very human interaction not only secures me with quick yet profound insights, but also relationships that often far outlast consulting projects.

ANALYSIS

This is a good failure essay in part because the main narrative does not have a happy ending. Many failure essays, in contrast, are really success stories told with a focus on the bumps along the road. In this case, the author is frank that he bungled his interaction with Adam. Although he does not say so directly, we can probably guess that he and Adam never had an especially productive working relationship (never mind that they did not become friends). As such, the essay is an example of a legitimate failure. When writing your own failure essay, do not waste time trying to sugarcoat a bad outcome. Say what happened and then move on.

The key, of course, is what the author learns from the experience. The answer: quite a lot. We see the author in a resilient light. He initially thinks he is not cut out for consulting but uses the experience to change his entire approach to interacting with clients. The result is a renewed focus on establishing relationships and building trust. The author has been humbled but emerges from the experience a more mature person and as someone skilled at working with senior-level executives. The ability to manage up in an organization as well as handle difficult conversations at all levels with both grace and candor will serve the author well at HBS and in his future career.

V. ETHICAL DILEMMA

Discuss an ethical dilemma that you experienced firsthand. How did you manage and resolve the situation?

This topic provides you with an opportunity to demonstrate your ability to make difficult choices in situations where your values are at odds with your obligations. Your essay should show how you think about gray areas in life where there is no clear right or wrong, how you approach issues of morality, and what your guiding principles are.

As the following examples demonstrate, ethical dilemmas can come in many forms and contexts. Some can be as simple as having to choose between telling the truth and lying, while others may have to do with conflicts between individual values and common practice in society. They can appear in the workplace and significantly impact people's careers or in the context of familial obligations where relationships are at stake. Regardless of the circumstances, however, they all are profound and serve as a test.

Making your essay successful requires more than just relating an anecdote. You must clarify what made a given situation an ethical dilemma and what made your decision so difficult. Why was it a test for you? Be sure to explain your thought process and the role of your personal ethics and beliefs. And do not shy away from being very honest and very personal. The point here is to share something fundamental about yourself, and you will not accomplish this without opening up your heart a little.

—Analisa Balares

Anonymous

I saw he was a banker from his pinstripes. I'd worked with bankers before, in Hong Kong. He flashed a smile.

"These numbers aren't going to work for us, son." I was sent back to "reevaluate" my projections.

It was the late '90s. The markets were buoyant, and dot-coms ruled. I was a consultant, working in Europe on a pre-IPO media company. With hindsight, floating as an online publisher was perhaps misjudged, but that was our mandate.

Working alongside bankers from a financial behemoth, we developed a model to value the company, before flotation in the U.S. and Europe. Because of the bank's deal structure, my firm had been brought in as an independent party to ratify the valuation. My responsibility was to develop a model to project the client's global businesses. I had spent two months researching, interviewing regional managers, and building the model.

Then the bankers arrived with a week of comp analysis. They suggested I alter my model to suit their estimations. They had the bigger picture, they assured me.

I was extremely uncomfortable. I told my manager I was under pressure to change my numbers, based on inadequate analysis. And this wasn't an internal business case, but a pre-IPO valuation; future shareholders would be affected. I told him I could not proceed this way with integrity. Unfortunately, I learned my team had an agenda; a technology venture was being discussed with the client. He suggested I proceed as instructed; after all, these were subjective forecasts. Balancing these considerations, whilst acknowledging there was no "right" answer, I compromised. I said I would produce two models; one with my original forecasts, and one with the bank's figures. I would hand over both models, but leave the decision with my superiors. I passed this by my mentor, and she agreed with my approach.

Later, my mentor assured me I had acted legally and ethically and she applauded my solution and interpersonal skills. The experience taught me you cannot always convince others to act honestly; however you must always play your role with integrity. With today's headlines of corporate misconduct, this message is more relevant than ever; I always ask myself: "How would my actions play on the *WSJ* front page?"

In conclusion, I honestly don't know which numbers they used. The stock opened at $8; a year on, it hovered at $8.

Note: certain identifying information has been changed to preserve confidentiality.

ANALYSIS

This essay is an interesting and instantly engaging story. The key to its success as an ethical dilemma essay, however, lies in the clear rendition of the core conflict between personal commitment to truth and the obligation to serve a client. We witness in detail the author's struggle to find a compromise between seemingly irreconcilable opposites. His manager's failure to resolve the dilemma makes the problem deeply personal.

The author uses this essay to demonstrate his strength of character and to provide an invaluable insight into his personal ethics. He comes across as someone who will not compromise his

V. Ethical Dilemma

integrity, and yet is pragmatic enough to understand that an outright refusal to adjust the forecasts would not resolve the issue (but most likely would have adverse professional consequences). There is little doubt that he is able to handle ethical dilemmas.

ANONYMOUS

I walked uneasily out of my colleague's office pondering the new competitor research project he had assigned me. Jorge had asked me to assume a false identity to facilitate data gathering in market interviews. He wanted to know all of the practices and pricing of our direct competitors.

I was uncomfortable employing these deceptive practices, but I failed to confront him. Was I naively blowing out of proportion a common business practice in Mexico? Did I have the right to apply my own ethical principles in a cultural environment with distinct norms and behaviors? Would it hinder my effectiveness if I did not follow typical local practices? Beleaguered with doubts, I delayed the calls, concentrating instead on background Internet research.

After several status inquiries from Jorge, I could not postpone the work any longer. At last, with a pit in my stomach, I dialed the first company. As the phone rang, I struggled to keep my "story" straight: my "pseudonym," my "company," and the accompanying contact information. At last I heard a voice. Perspiring and uneasy, I hung up the phone. Conducting sound business should not be this trying—my personal convictions won out.

I blocked out an appointment to meet with a former consultant of the competitor firm I had tried calling. It turned out that she was able to provide me with the same relevant and timely data I was seeking, without breaking her own confidentiality agreements. I quickly drew up a report of this company based on my in-house interview and Internet research. Armed with this deliverable and my reinforced convictions, I walked into Jorge's office.

I was frank with him about my discomfort at making the competitor calls under a false identity. Whether or not it was an accepted Mexican practice, I did not feel it was an ethically responsible activity for a large multinational consulting firm to be undertaking. I proposed my approach of using Internet tools and our colleagues to obtain as much legitimate data as possible, acknowledging the importance of this market intelligence for making product, pricing, and promotion decisions.

Though initially disappointed with my reticence, Jorge valued my openness and recognized the potential risks in his plan. He agreed to follow my alternate approach. Instead of hurting our relationship, it fostered greater confidence and respect. He knows he can count on me to get the job done—but he also knows I will stand up for my beliefs.

ANALYSIS

This essay is another example of the conflict between professional obligations and personal values. The issue is especially complicated because the ethically questionable professional conduct seems to be standard practice in Mexico. Someone else might have used this as a justification for compromising principles, but the author has an almost physical reaction to her first attempt at deception.

While the refusal to misrepresent herself attests to the strength of her convictions, it is the discovery of an alternative, ethically agreeable solution that proves her ability to attain desired objectives while working within the confines of her morality. Furthermore, the high level of detail and the honest description of the emotions involved make the story credible.

JAMES GANCOS

I was one of two consultants who conducted an independent assessment for a major financial services company. We were sponsored by its IT organization to assess the alignment of IT services to the various divisions and geographic locations of the business. During our assessment, we met with fifty of the top business leaders across four countries, including the CFO and CIO. We solicited their ideas for improvement and performed a statistical analysis of the results. When we shared the analysis with IT leadership, they asked us to remove some of the findings that reflected poorly upon their management practices before we reported the results to the business leaders.

Our dilemma was whether to report our independent findings to the business leaders against the wishes of IT leadership (who included our project sponsor) or to heed their request and dilute the findings. On the one hand, we reported to our project sponsor who paid our consulting fees and was our main contact at the company. On the other hand, we risked jeopardizing our credibility with the business leaders who had shared politically risky examples with us because they viewed the "independent" assessment as a vehicle for bringing about meaningful changes in the organization.

In order to address this dilemma, my colleague and I met to consider our options. Our reflection yielded one conclusion with two potential solutions. We concluded that all parties included in the assessment deserved to know the true findings of our study. As a result, we needed to either convince our sponsor that it was in his best interests to share the complete findings or find a way to show the limitations of the report's independence without alienating him.

Ultimately, both solutions were necessary. During meetings with our sponsor, we pointed out that the business leaders would clearly identify the withholdings, which would compromise IT's credibility. We also noted that omitting results would contradict the assessment's goal of bringing about constructive changes. Our sponsor accepted the validity of our arguments and reduced the number of omissions. However, since full disclosure was not an option for the IT organization, we also worked collaboratively with our sponsor to include a section in the presentation about the process used to conduct the assessment that clearly identified the input that IT leadership had to the results. This approach was ultimately satisfactory to IT leadership. It also provided the necessary flag to alert the business leaders to the withholdings from our final presentation.

ANALYSIS

This essay describes a dilemma that many consultants face: wanting to be honest in their assessment of a situation but not too honest so as to jeopardize future fees for the firm (and presumably bonuses for themselves). James writes a strong essay that clearly explains the problem and also the possible solutions. The structure is methodical and clear; you do not need to be familiar with consulting to understand the situation James faces. This is important. No matter what you plan to write about, you should assume that the reader may have very little knowledge about your company or industry.

James's solution demonstrates a high level of maturity. He is able to include at least some of the critical information but also makes it clear that the IT team influenced the presentation. James

V. Ethical Dilemma

comes across as trustworthy and conscientious. He recognizes who is paying his salary (the client) but he is equally mindful of his firm's reputation. The result appears to be a compromise that mostly satisfies everyone. It probably would have been worthwhile for James to include some information about how the story ultimately ended—did the IT department, for example, make any of the recommended changes, or was the consulting firm asked to conduct an additional project? Those details are not vital to the story, but would give the reader a better feel for how the story played out and if James was successful in helping the client.

Natalia Mlotok

It was a McKinsey project deep in the provinces of Russia. I had five client team members to manage. The team's initial ability to contribute was rather low as it often happens on out-of-town projects, but four team members caught up relatively quickly while one was constantly underperforming.

The obvious solution was to replace the underperforming team member. Project schedules are typically so tight that all team members should be strong performers. But this case was not so straightforward. The project got high visibility among the client's top managers. To replace the team member would have meant severe consequences for his career, not to say the end of it. On the other hand, my decision to keep him on the team, of course, would have resulted in increased workloads for other team members and especially for me.

First of all I tried to understand whether lack of skill or will was the reason for his underperformance, and when I realized he tried hard I decided to keep him on the team investing time in his development. At first I needed to help him gain back the respect of other team members. The latter figured out relatively quickly that the guy was delivering work of lower quality than they were and began to pick on him. The measures I took ranged from the direct interruption of the jokes to the demonstration of my own respect for him through asking his opinion before asking any of the others—listening attentively to what he had to say. Of course, these measures would not have had any success if they had not been supported by real improvements in the quality of his work. So, when the other team members were gone we were spending a couple of hours together discussing what he did well, what he could have done better, and what and how tasks should be done tomorrow. Gradually, the guy began to perform almost on par with the other team members.

I am still not sure it was the right decision. As I mentioned, the key decision-making factor for me was the team member's willingness to work hard to improve his performance. Someone else might argue that I would have added more value by focusing on developing top performers. I guess that is what a dilemma is about—there is no right or wrong decision, each person makes his own choice.

ANALYSIS

Natalia faces a difficult decision: keep a poorly performing consultant and jeopardize the project or remove him from the team and possibly end his tenure with the firm. The key for Natalia was that the young consultant appeared to be trying to improve. From this, we learn one way Natalia evaluates people and see her determination as she tries to help him get back on track. It is hard not to sympathize with the struggling consultant and to commend Natalia for taking him under her tutelage. We see Natalia as a teacher and mentor and as someone willing not only to give someone a second chance but also to defend that person in front of others, even though doing so could jeopardize her standing as leader of the project team. These are admirable qualities.

The crux of the essay is when Natalia wonders if she made the right decision. She admits that she is not sure if she did the right thing and explains how others could have viewed the situation differently. The last paragraph is in many ways the most interesting one. If there is anything that Natalia could have done to improve the essay, it would be to include a more detailed description of the

V. Ethical Dilemma

pros and cons of focusing on a poor performer versus developing the budding stars. She also could have discussed the merits of saving a coworker's career versus her team's obligation to the client. As it stands, the essay is an excellent story, but perhaps one that could focus slightly more on the dilemma itself rather than on what the author did to help a struggling coworker.

Anonymous

In a country where "gifts" are common, and every speedily obtained official form implies one, existence is simply the partial resolution of one ethical dilemma after another.

Recently, my driver's license expired and I had to renew it. Since mail orders for such routine matters do not exist, I made my way to the DMV on a day when I should have been at headquarters lobbying for a government permit. Unless one slips a note (worth about $2) to one of the young cadets, the wait is endless. If I choose to commit a small felony, I can leave in ten minutes. I refuse to pay such "gifts," so I waited, and five hours later, I left the DMV.

Paradoxically, such "gifts" are never considered bribes in my country. The reason is simple; a young government official's salary does not exceed $20 per month, so any "side" money is considered a contribution or a "gift." The personal example above is an everyday issue applicable to many government dealings.

Back at the office, the scene was different, but the situation was identical. My company, a pioneer resort owner, was building the first five-star hotel in a particular area. We were waiting for the last of a series of approvals and documents to release imported equipment from customs. Seven government permits were required, and six were on my desk. The city's local council, inexperienced in such business deals, delayed this essential final document. This would lead to unbudgeted expenses, and a long setback would hurt the financial viability of the project. The threat was clear. I knew what was required: send a carrier with a small fee of less than $100. With this incentive, I could release the goods, and not delay the project. I said "no" anyway. I explained my reasons to my boss who was already very anxious about the delay, and to my satisfaction, he complimented me. I retained a sense of freedom and moral integrity.

I continually discourage employees to pay petty "donations" to speed up their paperwork and impress their bosses. I would rather lose an entire project than damage the moral image of my country. Sometimes, the adherence to protocol can result in huge losses, but it is hardly comparable to forfeiting your own reputation and moral values.

ANALYSIS

The author of this essay tackles the challenge of adhering to his values in a country where common practice and common sense dictate the opposite. He opens with an effective one-sentence paragraph spelling out the essence of the issue: the dilemma is pervasive, requiring daily resolution. The specific examples are instrumental in conveying the scope of the problem. He is tested constantly by issues both large and small, yet the strength of his conviction wins every time.

The essay stands out because the author frames his ethical behavior not just as an individual choice but rather as an effort to impact the "moral image" of a nation. Given such stakes, it is clear that wasting a few hours waiting in line or losing a lucrative contract is a small price to pay. The applicant thus conveys not only his commitment to what is right, but also a profound sense of civic awareness and responsibility.

CINDY KO

I was working with a micro-finance institution that a U.S.-based Christian organization dedicated to development and relief work— helped establish in Kosovo. The organization in Kosovo is sustainable and financially independent, but its continuing legal affiliation with the U.S. organization makes it unclear whether its operations are, or should be, truly autonomous.

While the U.S. organization hires its employees exclusively from the Christian community, the group in Kosovo is not restricted by this requirement. I discovered, however, that the organization's hiring practices—relying on referrals from senior Christian staff—gave preferential treatment to members of the Christian community. It was unclear whether this preferential treatment in hiring was intentional, or whether it was even unethical. A private organization certainly had the right to hire whom it wished, did it not?

I felt uneasy in this ethical middle ground. Three main issues bothered me. First: These hiring practices went against our stated mission of promoting reconciliation between the Albanian and Serbian peoples, who have historically been divided along ethnic, linguistic, and *religious* lines. Second: Because we receive funds from donors, I felt we had an ethical obligation to use those funds (and tailor our practices) in accordance with the policies of the donor organizations. Preferential hiring based on religion ran contrary to the policies of a number of these donor organizations. Third: There appeared to be no set policy or standard within our own organization regarding hiring. Personnel and other policy matters seemed to change with the humor of each new director.

It was a difficult issue to broach with the director, not only because of its sensitivity, but also because I sensed that he might be using our paper affiliation with our parent organization to push his own religious agenda. I used our current search for a new loan officer as a starting point for a discussion of hiring practices. We had thus far interviewed only two, poorly qualified candidates—both employee referrals, and both from the Christian community. I expressed to him my concern about our limited applicant pool and suggested that all positions henceforth be advertised publicly in order to attract the most-qualified candidates and make the hiring process more transparent and equitable. He agreed. The following day I submitted the loan officer job description to the local newspaper. The response has been tremendous.

ANALYSIS

This essay is a great example of using a subtle ethical dilemma to illustrate multiple commendable traits of character. Initially Cindy is not even certain that an issue exists. She forces herself to dispassionately scrutinize the situation, thus demonstrating her strong ethical instinct. Her meticulous analysis attests to her ability to be objective even with emotionally charged matters. Her decision to take specific steps to counter the problem—rather than approach her director with a conversation about principles—is indicative of her political skill. Cindy shows that she is capable of identifying, analyzing, and resolving an ethical issue without ever provoking a potentially destructive confrontation. Her strong sense of morality and ability to take action are clearly conveyed.

The fact that the story takes place in Kosovo is interesting and

V. Ethical Dilemma

makes the essay stand out, but does not automatically create an ethical dilemma. If Cindy were faced with a similar issue in a corporate context and described her choices and actions in similar detail, the essay would have been equally effective.

ANONYMOUS

Is it ever appropriate to say "no" to your mother when she needs financial assistance? While I was growing up, this was not a concept I could ever fathom. My mother is a hardworking woman. No job has ever been beneath her when it came to supporting the family—whether it was loading luggage on airplanes or lifting packages at a shipping company. My mother was the infallible beacon of hard work, my superstar in a single parent household. Unfortunately, certain situations over the past three years have created an ethical dilemma in our relationship.

My love for my mother compelled me to eagerly enter the workforce in order to support her with supplemental income. However, her financial situation has deteriorated significantly over the past few years due to efforts to make up for shortfalls in her income by gambling at casinos. Her reliance on legal gambling has developed into borderline addiction. Due to inopportune losses, she has often turned to me for assistance in paying her rent and utility bills.

I tried to be supportive and encouraging by assisting her with creating a budget and getting her in touch with financial counselors. The situation has been emotionally difficult for me, as her requests for money have increased. While I consider myself to be financially responsible and disciplined, it is difficult for me to continue feeling comfortable supporting her behavior through passive measures. I often fear that my assistance may be more detrimental than helpful. As a resolution, I recently tried declining her continued requests for financial assistance. Of course, I cannot make such a decision without fierce internal conflict and in the end, I simply felt guilty for saying "no."

I have given her the money that she needed on every occasion. I do so because I realize that everything that I have attained in my career is in large part due to her unconditional love and support. Under normal circumstances, I would not hesitate to support her financially, but this situation is troubling because I am also the source of the family's long-term financial stability. Realistically, I must think in terms of my own future, as I have no one to turn to in case of a financial emergency of my own. While I have yet to discover a final resolution to this ongoing dilemma, what I have found is that while in some situations, I should say "no" to my mother, I have a moral obligation to provide her with a supportive network, just as she did for me when I was a child.

ANALYSIS

The author of this piece shares a very personal problem. Simply identifying the issue, however, would be insufficient to make this essay meaningful. Its strength is derived from the detailed account of arriving at the author's final decision. The list of failed attempts to improve her mother's financial planning ability clarifies how reluctantly she is resorting to this extreme measure. The complexity of the feelings involved is self-evident.

The author's deep awareness of the consequences regardless of her course of action shows that despite the tremendously emotional nature of the situation she is able to find sufficient distance to consider rationally the alternatives. Her ability to maintain a longer-term perspective demonstrates an unusual level of maturity. Thus, the essay is more than just a story that elicits empathy; it is a testament to the author's integrity and strength of character.

Anonymous

Note: All names, including the school name, have been changed to preserve confidentiality.

In high school, a teacher began writing me letters that became increasingly inappropriate as the year passed. He had been my most intellectually engaging teacher, and I had chosen him as an independent-study advisor in my senior year. Most indiscretions occurred during these sessions. It took me time to acknowledge the situation, but eventually, I considered reporting him. Oddly, I feared for his job and worried even more for the well-being of his son, who was also a student at my school. Because Addington waived tuition for teachers' children, if this teacher were fired, his son, on top of his personal suffering, would have lost his seat. The situation was further complicated as his son, Joe, was my younger brother's friend. Though the letters disturbed me, having grown up in a supportive family and community, I was able to compartmentalize them as the misgivings of an unfulfilled man. Though I was torn about coming forward, I decided to protect Joe by remaining silent.

The events stayed with me through my first year in college, and by Thanksgiving, I realized that I had made the wrong decision. Not understanding the dilemma I had faced, I thought I had picked between defending myself and adversely altering the life of my brother's friend. In high school, I believed that I had acted selflessly to preserve Joe's adolescent experience. However, by not coming forward, I realized I had put other women attending Addington at risk. Yet, as Joe was still a student there, the dilemma I faced was

115

between protecting other potential victims at Addington and preserving Joe's welfare.

I decided I had to speak to the headmaster. Walking into his office during Thanksgiving break, I still hoped to preserve Joe's remaining seven months. My plan was to speak with Mr. Smith about sexual harassment broadly at Addington. I told him that I did not want to reveal specific events, but that it was a widespread problem. As a solution, I volunteered to work with him to set community standards on sexual harassment. The goal would be to get every teacher to sign a contract agreeing to these standards and to communicate them throughout the school. Though Mr. Smith pushed for examples, I was able to convince him that the problem existed without revealing details. The sexual harassment community standards were instituted by February. Joe graduated Addington, and his father left the school shortly afterwards.

ANALYSIS

The author of this essay bravely shares an extremely personal experience. The seriousness of the subject matter makes her essay instantly memorable. However, simply sharing a traumatic episode would be insufficient. What makes the essay truly stand out is the extent to which the author's character and personal values are conveyed in the story.

For instance, her desire to protect other women in her high school, even after she has moved on to college, is indicative of her deep commitment to ethics, not just in her own life, but in society at large. While most people would probably elect to forget about the unpleasant experience, she cannot knowingly allow others to remain at risk.

Another aspect of her character that can be gleaned is a will-

V. Ethical Dilemma

ingness to admit mistakes—a very difficult skill in the context of emotionally charged ethical dilemmas. Deciding that "doing nothing" was the wrong choice is indicative of the author's high degree of honesty, especially with herself. Finally, her approach to taking action while avoiding an outright confrontation with the perpetrator attests to her poise in handling difficult situations.

VI. THREE ACCOMPLISHMENTS

What are your three most substantial accomplishments, and why do you view them as such?

This is one of those essays that is probably a permanent fixture in the HBS application. The other essays evolve a bit from year to year but count on this one always being there. This is a chance to supplement themes already mentioned in the other essays and also to sneak in something completely new about yourself that is not evident elsewhere.

Think of the question as an opportunity to provide three snapshots of yourself. Although there are no set rules, most applicants target approximately two hundred words per accomplishment and pick accomplishments from three different areas of their lives. Many essays adhere to a boilerplate format of one extracurricular accomplishment, one academic accomplishment, and one career accomplishment, but do not feel that you have to follow this formula.

You may be wondering whether your accomplishments are significant enough. Is winning the gold metal in the Olympics or saving a child from a burning building substantial? Sure, but not every HBS student can lay claim to such feats. In fact, few can. The key—illustrated by the essays that follow—is to explain *why* you view your accomplishments as important.

In sharing these stories, applicants often have a hard time deciding what is too personal or what happened too long ago. As the included examples demonstrate, there are many angles that can work, and you should not limit yourself to such topics as work and school life.

—Ling Hu

DANIEL LEWIS

1

My most substantial accomplishment was my recovery from a motorcycle accident on September 9, 1996, my junior year at Tufts. On the way to Harvard Square, a drunk driver swerved in front of my oncoming motorcycle. My legs collided with the roof of her car, and I was catapulted through the air at over forty miles per hour, landing headfirst on the asphalt. I awoke from surgery eighteen hours later with four lacerated nerves and titanium rods securing my shattered femur, radius, ulna, and hand.

Following two weeks in the hospital, the orthopedic surgeon predicted I'd never have full use of my hand again, and suggested that I go to a special rehab clinic in California. "Rehab will fix my bones, but my brain will turn to mush," I thought. I phoned school the next day to find out which of my classes were wheelchair accessible. I spent the next semester wheeling through the Boston winter to physical therapy three times a day while studying astronomy and Russian.

It was the most painful, and challenging, time of my life. At graduation two years later, I was awarded Tufts's Ellen C. Myers Award for "outstanding scholarship in the face of adverse circumstances." The next day, I went back to Mass. General, and did four cartwheels across my doctor's office—never say never.

2

Next is the BroadbandCompass, a software program conceived in the basement of a nondescript building in a Denver-area business park. My five partners and I had only a dream, plus hand-me-down hardware and a few free ninety-day evaluation licenses for Web server software. We outlined the framework for our platform. Two years of strategy work at MediaOne Cable had convinced us it was time somebody made finding a broadband connection online as easy as finding a book on Amazon.com.

Funded with about a nickel over a million dollars, we labored for two years in that basement writing software code and convincing America's largest access providers, electronics retailers, and Web portals that our platform would change the way people looked for Internet access. We drudged through the Internet boom and the dot-com bust. But we made it. Today, our tool is leveraged by industry giants such as Office Depot, Gateway, Microsoft, CompUSA, Circuit City, and numerous others. I am proud to say I wrote Product Specification V.1.0 for the technology that's helped one in ten Internet users find a broadband connection.

3

I am proud of my music. I have been obsessed with entertaining large crowds ever since I first laid hands on a pair of turntables in high school. I began my career as a bilingual "turntablist" my senior year abroad at a nightclub called Taxman in Moscow. Since then, I have developed a repertoire that includes gigs in some of Europe's and America's largest nightclubs, including sellout crowds of more than two thousand people. I enjoy convincing critics that mixing records is an art form, not just aimless basement shenanigans. Following the abrupt demise of a nightclub venture in 1998 (see "failure" question for details), I founded Amazing Productions, Inc., a mobile disc jockey service. Though entertaining has never been my full-time occupation, it has always been my full-time passion. My knack for technology gives Amazing Productions a competitive advantage in the Denver market, as our shows have become known for their array of high-tech marvels. These range from blends of musical media—including vinyl, CDs, and MP3s—to computer-driven acoustics, lasers, and special effects. We have operated profitably since Q1 99, and have since become a household name in the Denver DJ industry. Check us out at www.amazingdj.com.

ANALYSIS

Daniel's essay is a winner because it is both substantive and stylish. He displays a dynamic personality not only through his achievements but also through his vibrant prose. His action-packed writing captivates the reader with colorful adjectives and striking descriptions.

Daniel is a memorable candidate because he is able to show rather than tell. His four cartwheels across his doctor's office display not only literary but also physical dexterity. He faces obstacles with humor and humility and paints himself as a fighter, not only through personal tragedy but also in the world of business. His diverse interests are captured with references to astronomy and Russian, programming and technology and his passion for music. This essay stands out because the author comes across as an impressive personality and someone you want to get to know more deeply. That is a winning combination you may want to keep in mind when crafting your own text.

ERIK JOHNSON

The three most substantial accomplishments in my life comprise an athletic, a personal, and a professional accomplishment. These accomplishments have rewarded me with confidence in myself and my abilities, because they proved to me that I was capable of successfully handling difficult challenges.

The first accomplishment was the Pedro Zamora National College Bike Tour. I was one of five college students who organized, arranged financing for, and completed a cross-country bicycle tour from Los Angeles to Boston. We spoke at twenty-seven colleges with the objective of raising awareness on college campuses about the threat that HIV poses to college students. In Washington, D.C., we were received at the White House by First Lady Hillary Clinton. Additionally, we raised over $50,000 from corporate sponsors for HIV prevention education. I consider the tour to be one of my most rewarding accomplishments in terms of the physical and organizational challenges as well as the thought that we might have encouraged someone to behave differently and thereby, potentially avoid contracting HIV. The trip also taught me how to push myself and my teammates to perform beyond our abilities as individuals.

The second accomplishment was living and working abroad for three and a half years. I knew that I wanted to travel the world and have a career in international business. I just did not know where to start or how to gain experience. I tried to obtain a job overseas while still in school but ran into the problem that I did not have any significant work experience. I almost decided to give up and wait until later in my career to work overseas. But, something in my mind pushed me to take the risk and go for it. After graduating from college, I traveled in Australia and Africa for three months. When I ran low on money, I went to London in search of a job. Fortunately, I quickly found a job as an analyst for a firm based in Switzerland. I was soon transferred to the Swiss headquarters and then on to Chile. Over those three and a half years, I traveled to forty countries on six continents, gained significant international work experience, and learned a great deal about myself from exposure to new ideas and situations.

The third accomplishment results from a work experience. In June 1999, the company I worked for transferred me from Switzerland to Chile to conduct a survey of the Chilean market for a particular chemical used in the copper refining process. If the market proved to be attractive, the company planned to construct a $2 million local production facility. My role was to develop a business model including market size and price structure, production costs and a return on investment analysis to determine whether the plant would be successful or not.

I was somewhat daunted by the task, since a $2 million decision would be made based on my evaluation of the project. Over the course of six months, I met with the majority of our potential customers in order to produce a detailed market survey, found a suitable piece of property to locate the plant, worked with local engineering firms to develop plant construction costs, and produced a detailed production cost model based on market factors. After completing my analysis, I successfully recommended that the project not be pursued because of an unacceptably low return. This project offered me a significant level of responsibility, and I am pleased that I was able to meet such a tough professional challenge.

VI. Three Accomplishments

ANALYSIS

Erik does a nice job here by seamlessly weaving together three stories. His colorful and detail-rich writing brings his accomplishments to life and results in a superb essay that goes beyond just saying something is good and instead proves it to you. As with many essays in this section, that is the key: convincing the reader that what you did is important to you, not that it is important in its own right. This may seem like a subtle point but it is worth remembering. Playing a tiny role in a $500 million deal but not having much to say other than that it was a big deal is a lot less meaningful than Erik's description of a relatively small project, but one where he had a major impact. Gaudy numbers matter less than what you did or what you learned. It is inevitable that someone else will have worked on a bigger deal so try not to win based on size alone.

Erik comes across as courageous and curious and as an individual you would want to sit next to on a long flight. Key to this is the tone of the essay, which is accessible, matter-of-fact, and not at all arrogant (always a risk when writing about things that you have done well).

Martin Brand

Four years after I had initially set myself the goal, I succeeded in winning the National Mathematics Competition in Germany. Seeing prolonged struggle turn into eventual success makes this one of my most valuable achievements. It helped me form an "it can be done" attitude that has stayed with me ever since. I first learned of the competition during a summer program in 1990 where I met some former finalists. The following year, when I was on exchange in the U.S., I had the competition materials sent over from Germany. I made it though the first two rounds to become one of seventy finalists invited to a weekend where the five national winners would be chosen. I wasn't one of them. The following year I again advanced to the finals only to fail at the last test. I continued to work on my skills and when I made it to the finals for the third time in a row, I knew it was my last chance. I had to survive a grilling by university professors on an unknown topic, but this time I could solve every problem. Walking out of the interview I knew I had won. Three days later the letter arrived. It was a dream come true.

An accomplishment of a different kind is my work as an ambulance driver, which I chose as an alternative to military service. After gaining a qualification as a paramedic I started to man ambulances in my hometown near Düsseldorf. I worked both in supervised medical transports between hospitals and in emergency situations. My strongest memory is of the death of a child when we hit a traffic jam and could not make it to the hospital in time. I was in the back of the car with the boy and his mother. I never felt more helpless in my life. But there are also many happy memories, of the people whom we succeeded in helping during emergencies and of the many grateful patients on our regular transport services. During the fifteen months on the ambulances I matured tremendously. I learned to take on responsibility for other people when they needed me the most. I dealt with extreme pressure and human tragedy. These were enormous challenges to overcome. But every day I was also able to experience how gratifying helping others can be. I view my time on the ambulances as an achievement because I was able to learn and grow, but more importantly for the help we were able to provide to the patients and the community.

My third achievement is having a significant impact on the trading strategies of the currency options group at Goldman Sachs. I began developing my own pricing spreadsheets soon after I joined the group. Being in the privileged position of combining a strong mathematical background with the practical grasp of the market that our "rocket scientist" developers lacked, I was able to arrive at several innovations. Whilst some enthusiastically supported my work (it would not have been possible otherwise), I encountered opposition from senior members of the group who lacked the younger traders' quantitative background and feared that eventually innovation would undermine their power base. I persevered, using my trading portfolio as a trial ground. Eventually, the better ideas prevailed and my interpolation now forms the basis of the strategy that group uses to identify value in the market. I am proud of having had the spirit and ability to innovate our strategies, but it is the strength to carry on in the face of adversity that makes this my biggest professional achievement to date.

VI. Three Accomplishments

ANALYSIS

Do not fall into the trap of thinking you have to come across as Hercules. It is great if you can, but such answers are neither realistic nor necessary. In the case of this essay, Martin shows maturity and humility by admitting his weaknesses and acknowledging how others helped him accomplish his goals. These traits make him notable.

Martin describes how he handles adversity. Accomplishment for him is a process of overcoming failures and setbacks; his stories would not have the same impact if he had won the mathematics competition on the first try or had saved every person in his ambulance. He does not dwell on these setbacks, though, and instead focuses on how he overcame them. As a reader you are left remembering his "it can be done" attitude.

Martin chooses to arrange his accomplishments in chronological order. This works well because the themes of the first story resonate in the second and the third. Again, this level of coherence is not necessary, but adds to this essay's overall effectiveness.

ANONYMOUS

I wrote my first short story at eight. It was five pages long and truly awful. But it was too late; I loved writing. Since then I have written innumerable stories and four feature-film screenplays.

The Big Deal was my fourth script, set in the world of high finance. It's a comedy, based on the concept of floating the UK on the stock exchange; its satirical backbone is from my own firsthand corporate experience.

Why is this an accomplishment? It's my best writing to date. It's been short-listed for a European Union development fund. It's been optioned by a production company. It's currently at a global talent agency as a showcase script.

Screenwriting is the most collaborative writing medium, with a strong team element (from producers to editors and directors) and I approach it with no less rigor or commitment than my job; neither are they mutually exclusive, as I work in consulting to media companies. Every time I write, it's a new challenge, finding solutions to creative problems. I pour my heart and energies into it. I have trekked the Himalayas and the Andes, but I'm most proud of my little mountain of scripts. It's my character on a page.

Two years ago, I worked on the pan-European launch of Sony's next-generation console, PlayStation 2. Using statistical programs, I crafted customer segmentations and designed marketing campaigns, capitalizing on Accenture's technological solutions. Additionally, I helped develop a retail strategy to ensure maximum customer data-capture.

As a strategy consultant, it is rare to see a project from conception to implementation. However, on this job, I worked for months before the launch and witnessed the product's phenomenal success. This was the largest-ever consumer electronics launch in Europe, and in the UK alone, one in five households has a PlayStation.

After two years of working as a consultant at Accenture, this was the first time I had been given real responsibility to lead a workstream. Presenting my work to senior executives at Sony, my contribution was met with huge client satisfaction and my company rewarded me with a promotion. Additionally, the industry captivated me as an area that blends technology with artistry and commerce. For the first time I experienced the fusion of creativity and enterprise. Media and entertainment; I'd found my industry.

This year, I traveled to a Bosnian orphanage on charitable leave. Inspired by the book *Welcome to Sarajevo*, I decided to travel there to see those left behind. I found a crumbling institution, packed with children, some mentally and physically abused. The building had been shelled during the war and some had seen their parents murdered. But I was inspired by the love and commitment of the charity's staff. They coped as best they could, surviving on imagination and resilience. I interviewed them, took photographs and promised to help them.

Back home, I worked with the charity to draft a proposal to Accenture, structuring the messages to ensure maximum impact within my organization, and I lobbied key executives. We secured $40,000. I have since been invited by the charity to Rwanda and Sierra Leone.

I take great pride in this achievement. I made the journey just before my father died. As British ambassador, he had dedicated his life to bringing security to strangers around the world. He didn't always understand my work as a consultant; however, after my trip I knew he was so proud. He saw I had used the resources available to me to realize change.

VI. Three Accomplishments

This experience has grown my desire to build a lasting partnership between the charity and Accenture, fostering a culture of corporate responsibility.

ANALYSIS

This applicant lures in the reader by painting a picture of a young boy scribbling untrained handwriting with his feet dangling from a high office chair. The author's critique of his work is honest but funny (of course the story was awful—he was eight years old!) and is a good way to break the ice; you can tell he does not take himself too seriously.

From there, both substance and literary gems keep the essay alive. The author avoids sounding trite and is able to convey his passion for writing: "I have trekked the Himalayas and the Andes, but I'm most proud of my little mountain of scripts." In crafting the story, he anticipates the reader's question, "Why come to business school, why not be a writer?" He addresses this by pointing to a key similarity between business and writing, namely the task of finding creative solutions to problems. The essay is another example of weaving consistent themes through all three accomplishments. The author does this beautifully; the three stories are quite different but similar enough that we begin to see a picture of a larger person emerge.

ANONYMOUS

CEO of Company S: Selling a vision to others

One of my biggest accomplishments occurred in 1999, when I turned my vision into a reality, creating a company called Company S. I bootstrapped the company with an initial $14,000 from our first client and over the course of two years, grew the company to a team of eighteen employees. Eventually we raised a first round of financing, expanded our presence into six U.S. cities, and opened our first international office in India, which alone generated $240,000 in new sales over a two-week period. We also created a client list of over one hundred and fifty companies, received free marketing press from more than twenty publications, and faced the opportunity of modifying our business model in a changing economy.

This is an accomplishment in my eyes because I was able to communicate a vision to others, creating a client list of over one hundred and fifty clients despite the fact that we were an inexperienced start-up with a zero-dollar marketing budget. Since we could not afford to advertise, I quickly realized that the best marketing was free press. Articles published in the *Harbus*, *CNET*, and *Boston* magazine gave us the much-needed credibility as we went to sell our services. I was able to sign up companies such as Scient, McKinsey, and Epinions, creating an environment where my employees were inspired and sacrificed higher salaries and worked late hours to help the company reach our goals. Through this experience I realized that by thinking creatively and providing others with a vision, I could be successful.

The Family: Teamwork through rough times

When my father lost his job as a chemical engineer in the 1980s recession, my parents purchased a Laundromat to help pay the bills. During this period, it was essential that our family act as a team both at home and at work. At home, my brother and I split the household chores of laundry, gardening, and cleaning. At work, my brother and father maintained washers and dryers, while my mother and I handed out change, loaded vending machines, and purchased supplies. Every Sunday after finishing my homework, I would spend hours rolling quarters. This experience strengthened our family as a unit. I view this as an accomplishment because I learned the importance of communication and teamwork during tough times. I also gained critical time management skills since I had to balance schoolwork, extracurricular activities, chores, friends, and the business. Finally, this experience taught me the business fundamentals and developed my social skills through my interactions with employees and customers. This experience taught me invaluable skills and laid the foundation for the person I am today.

Advisor for Micro-Enterprise Organization: Giving back to community

In late 2000, I became an advisor for a Bay Area micro-enterprise organization aimed at providing business and technical training to low-income Asian-American women who are starting small businesses. This is a substantial accomplishment for three reasons. First, as a result of my helping the organization define its mission and business plan, it was named a winner in the Craigslist Nonprofit Competition (similar to the private sector Spring Board Venture Capital Award). Second, I am able to serve as an entrepreneurial mentor to women pursuing their visions. Although I was fortunate to have my mother as a mentor, I wished there had been more women role models when starting my own company. In addition, due to my role, the executive director of another organization, an international nonprofit utilizing the digital economy to empower the poor, contacted me to head up their Boston chapter in 2002. By collaborating with these organizations as an advisor, I am influencing both the executive directors and the communities they serve.

Note: Certain identifying information has been changed to preserve confidentiality.

ANALYSIS

The author begins with an impressive story about how she created a company from nothing. The reader is flooded with facts and figures that paint an impressive picture of a young entrepreneur. The key is that the author does not stop there—she goes on to say not just what she did but how she did it. She shows her street smarts by writing about her realization that the best marketing was free press. She demonstrates her ability to inspire by pointing to her employees' willingness to sacrifice higher pay and personal time to join her company.

In choosing to place the story about her upbringing second, the author steps back chronologically but still moves the essay forward because she reveals why she is who she is now. Her third accomplishment about her contributions to the community shows that she is socially aware and completes the picture of a well-rounded young leader.

Michael Kerlin

Finding my Irish Heritage

I've never felt more fulfilled than when I visited my family's ancestral home in Ireland for the first time. In my diverse international experiences, I had never directly encountered my own family's rich cultural heritage. So, after years of playing the Irish fiddle and listening to my granny's stories of Uncle Johnny the fiddler, I traveled to the very farm where my granny grew up. I played soccer with cousins I had only seen in pictures, visited my great-grandfather's grave, and saw the schoolhouse where my granny completed her second-grade education.

After showing me around the farm, my cousins insisted on finding me a fiddle to play. The local musician happened to have just restored Uncle Johnny's fiddle. We borrowed it and I played "Shoe the Donkey" and other favorites on my great-great-granduncle's fiddle. The emotion of playing this fiddle was tremendous—it embodied a physical and emotional connection between past and present—yet it fell far short of the joy I felt in recounting the story to my granny. As a result of my family pilgrimage, my granny left this world two years later knowing that Uncle Johnny's legacy was alive and well.

McKinsey: From Consulting to Operations

During my second year at McKinsey, I led a four-person client team through a successful home heating oil-marketing pilot that convinced me that I could be a manager and not just a consultant.

The week before the pilot, the client team leader Gerry got called out of town. Having led the pilot design, I was the natural selection to manage the first week of the rollout from Gerry's office. Dedication and integrity earlier in the project gave me the organizational credibility to assume the role of manager, which was essential for the successful execution of the tasks at hand. I worked with Gerry's five-person staff to organize and analyze the early pilot results, fielded questions from twenty-six branch managers, sent out daily updates, and coached managers who were falling behind. As operational glitches emerged, I mobilized the necessary corporate departments to develop quick solutions. During that first week of the pilot, I helped a two-hundred-and-fifty-person organization realize its potential to implement a project rapidly and effectively. At the same time, I discovered my own ability to manage and execute at the helm of a large operation.

Personal Impact in Portugal

In 1997, I won a Fulbright Scholarship to study African immigration to Portugal. Despite the relaxed requirements of the program, I defined my own rigorous framework for the year. I identified a gap in the current literature on immigrant transnationalism and focused my research on Guinea-Bissauan immigrants' efforts to support development projects in their home villages. My work was subsequently published in the journal of *South European Society & Politics*.

Publishing my research was a tangible measure of my achievements in Portugal, yet for me success was demonstrated by the personal impact that I had on the very immigrants I was researching. I created and led volunteer English classes for African college students and started a community youth center's first-ever physical education program. As a measure of the trust I developed with the community, I was asked to serve as a *portador*, or courier of money and material goods from immigrants to their families, during my field research trip to Guinea-Bissau. In doing so, I was able to connect immigrants with their families only three months before they lost all contact due to the outbreak of civil war in Guinea-Bissau. These unique personal contributions transformed intellectual endeavor into action and no doubt informed my larger transition from consultant to nonprofit manager two years later.

ANALYSIS

Michael takes the reader through three events in his life, each leading to self-discovery. In selecting a personal pilgrimage, a business pilot, and a volunteering experience, he gives the reader three views into what is important to him.

In the first story, Michael juxtaposes his diverse international experiences with his long-overdue pilgrimage to a small town in Ireland and then describes the impact this had on his grandmother. In the second story, Michael says that while others may see the external success of the pilot project, his personal reward came from discovering his leadership abilities. In the third story, Michael describes how he is proud of his work as a Fulbright scholar, not because he was published, but instead because of the impact he had on immigrants' lives. All three stories are excellent not just because they are impressive in their own right, but because Michael tells the reader why his accomplishments are important to him personally. The lesson here is not to assume that your accomplishments will shine without a meaningful and personal context. While what you have accomplished may be impressive, the value here is in helping the admissions committee learn what is important to you.

ANONYMOUS

The Yale Daily News (YDN)

As publisher and president of the *Yale Daily News*, I led the organization to record profits. I introduced a new source of revenue by negotiating a landmark contract with Simon & Schuster to publish five reference books for high school and college students. I also revamped the circulation of the paper, creating a more cost-effective system. Lastly, I recruited a larger sales force, leading to stronger advertising sales. The increased profits enabled us to introduce color printing and an expanded daily paper and to contribute to the *YDN*'s endowment for the first time in a decade.

I consider my tenure as publisher and president of the *Yale Daily News* a substantial accomplishment for several reasons. Without any formal business education, I led the organization to new heights while balancing other leadership positions. While publisher, I worked forty hours per week at the *YDN*. Despite this significant time commitment, I successfully served as president of my sorority and senior society and organized a tutoring program. In order to manage the *YDN* and my other responsibilities, I learned how to prioritize tasks, delegate projects, and manage others.

I cherish my experience as publisher of the *YDN* because it demonstrated to me my ability to lead effectively and shaped my professional aspirations to run an organization.

Competitive Intelligence

When I began working in Morgan Stanley's retail brokerage division, I was shocked by the dearth of competitor and industry knowledge. We could not improve our business model without better understanding industry trends and our position relative to the competition.

After identifying this gap, I conceived *Competitive Intelligence*, a biweekly newsletter designed to detail competitor news and industry trends. I created a template, determined my audience, selected appropriate categories of news, and identified relevant news sources. I presented my business case and a sample issue to the division's president. He immediately approved the program. From the initial issue, the feedback was overwhelmingly positive. The distribution of *Competitive Intelligence* has grown from fifteen to one thousand employees since the newsletter's introduction, demonstrating its relevance and success.

I am proud of my efforts to establish *Competitive Intelligence* because I successfully identified a need within the division, developed an appropriate tool to fill the need, and have consistently executed a quality product. As a result of *Competitive Intelligence*, senior management is more knowledgeable about our competitive position, and I am often consulted as the resident expert on the competition. However, I take the greatest pride in the initiative I took to create *Competitive Intelligence* and consider that the true accomplishment.

Student/Sponsor Partners (S/SP)

In September 2000, through S/SP, I began sponsoring Kimberly, a high school freshman from the Bronx. While I immediately liked Kim, we struggled to connect. Nonetheless, I faithfully called Kim every two weeks to monitor her adjustment to high school. I closely followed her academic progress and provided her with supplementary study materials. During the school year, we met every six weeks. Hoping that Kim would share more about herself, I exposed Kim to some of my interests, such as visiting art exhibits and museums. Gradually, as I demonstrated my commitment and friendship to her, Kim opened up. Today, we have established a true bond and are important parts of one another's lives. I am proud to serve as a positive role model for Kim. Although the academic and financial support I provide is critical to Kim's academic success, I consider my dedication and loyalty to Kim the most noteworthy accomplishment.

These three accomplishments highlight four qualities I value highly: leadership, initiative, dedication, and loyalty.

ANALYSIS

This essay is remarkably well organized and clear. In a highly systemic way, the author discusses each of her three accomplishments by first describing the situation and then providing a candid assessment of why the achievement was important. Thus, the essay exhaustively addresses the core of the question.

Pushing a highly structured approach to an extreme can be a little dangerous, however. The author chooses to adhere to the standard trio of extracurricular, professional, and community service achievements seen in many other essays. When combined with the repetitive structure (accomplishment-explanation), the accomplishments run the risk of losing some of their luster. Fortunately, in this case there is enough substance in each of the anecdotes to overshadow the cliché structure, and content triumphs over form.

DALE SCHILLING

The Japanese language is highly complex. Two alphabets and a large number of kanji (characters) must be memorized, and respect for one's elders reflected in the grammar itself: to mistake this is to risk insult. At age seventeen, after five years of study at high school in Australia, I came to Japan with a few rudimentary phrases and four hundred kanji—the average Japanese high school student knows more than two thousand.

My move to Japan in April 1993 represented a great academic challenge—to attend lectures, research, and study under the same conditions as a native at a Japanese university—but also a personal opportunity, a tremendous chance to broaden my horizons. Five years in a foreign country and culture by myself was a daunting prospect, but I took the view that if I could not cope, I could always return to Australia fluent in Japanese after the one-year intensive language training course. The experience was both more challenging and rewarding than I had imagined.

The first year at Kyoto University was particularly tough academically. Although Japanese language school prepared me for the grammar and vocabulary needed, I was overwhelmed at first by the sheer amount of work required, taking two hours, for example, to read what took my Japanese classmates half an hour. Not only was I studying new concepts, but in a foreign language; a novel experience was to learn German and Chinese from a Japanese base. It was slow and painstaking work. However, I refused to give up, setting myself arbitrary high standards. I used English books to study together with the Japanese texts, borrowed friends' notes to fill in the gaps I had missed in lectures, and with perseverance my language ability and grades improved.

At university, a classmate asked me to join a newly established amateur musical drama group. I had performed in musicals and youth operas in Australia and was keen to join. We did everything ourselves, from creating the dialogue (in Japanese), music and dance routines, to backstage work (making costumes, sets, and lighting), to ticketing and marketing. The first performance had an audience of only one hundred in a crude yet intimate setting, but with time our productions increased in scale and hugely improved in quality. My strength is singing, and I am particularly proud that the vocal training regimens I implemented helped the group cope with the acoustics of the increasingly larger venues. I was also rapt when after one production I received a message addressed to the "foreign-looking detective" complimenting my performance. By my senior year, the group's performance was an established part of the Kyoto University Students' Festival, in a hall seating over one thousand people.

Upon graduation, I decided to work for a Japanese trading company. Many foreign students return home at that stage claiming some expertise in Japanese culture, but I realized I lacked the needed experience in Japanese business culture. I entered the company—only the second Westerner to do so—with much the same attitude that I had five years earlier: I have nothing to lose.

From the beginning I was treated no differently, expected to perform to the level of my peers. I appreciated and accepted the challenge, and I believe rose to it. Not only have I come to understand Japanese customs—reporting techniques and the etiquette required in business discussions, for example—but also the Japanese way of thinking. However, this has not been to the detriment to my Western side. I believe I have maintained a global perspective and balance between cultures necessary for international business.

VI. Three Accomplishments

ANALYSIS

Rather than presenting three independent accomplishments, Dale writes a narrative of his decision to study and eventually work in Japan. While moving to a foreign country is probably not all that unusual in its own right (lots of applicants do this), Dale sets the stage by explaining why Japan, in particular, was such a challenging place to live and study. From all three stories we learn that he is determined and persistent and willing to do whatever it takes to make the most of a daunting situation. While he concedes that he could easily have gone home if Japan did not work out, we come to see that Dale is someone who would never have given up until he had accomplished what he had set out to do.

The third accomplishment is perhaps the least compelling because while it reinforces that Dale approaches new situations with an open mind and a lot of determination, it does not say much about what he contributed to the organization. The essay would end on a stronger note if Dale had written about that rather than finishing with a somewhat confusing line about how living in Japan was not a "detriment" to his Australian heritage.

On the whole, though, this is an excellent example of an essay that weaves three accomplishments into a cohesive narrative and serves as a good contrast to the more traditionally structured essays that describe a series of largely independent achievements.

VII. STRENGTHS AND WEAKNESSES

Provide a candid assessment of your strengths and weaknesses.

As with other essays topics, the first step in writing about your strengths and weaknesses is to have a clear assessment of who you are. Although it may be difficult to be your "biggest fan" and at the same time be your "worst critic," this essay topic provides you with a focused opportunity to prove that you know yourself. It is important that you be quite frank. Do not resort to false modesty and do not brag. Do not be shy, but be very honest.

While you probably will not have too much trouble listing your strengths, you may at first have trouble writing about your weaknesses. However, think of it as an opportunity to demonstrate your personal and professional development, either past or future. Choose a weakness (not a disguised strength) and clearly illustrate how you became aware of it. Show how it has affected your life and share how you have tried to overcome it. This way, the reader will see you as mature and self-aware. On the other hand, be careful not to choose weaknesses that will hinder your ability to succeed in business school: for example, a fear of public speaking.

The following essays demonstrate the diversity of methods for conveying strengths and weaknesses. Using specific anecdotes to back up your self-assessment tends to work best, although a list of traits and characteristics can also be effective if employed creatively. Your writing style can be formal or conversational, analytical or literary, as long as you deliver your message with confidence and sincerity. Note that in the best examples, the form reflects and backs up the content.

Finally, remember that although you are assessing your character, you are also implicitly making a case for admission to HBS. If you can position your strengths as future contributions to the school community and your weaknesses as development needs that can be addressed by the MBA program, your essay will be difficult to overlook.

—LaMonica Carpenter

ELIZABETH DE SAINT-AIGNAN

Above all, I am passionate. I hunger for knowledge and truth. I follow through with reading and debate until I am satisfied with my level of understanding. I learn quickly. I integrate disparate concepts with relative ease. I avoid jumping to conclusions. Once convinced, I will fight for my point of view. Once proven wrong, I am equally happy to accept the opposing conclusion. When I cannot find the answer, or I know that another would excel where I am weak, I am quick to recognize my limitations and seek assistance. These strengths enable me to problem-solve efficiently and completely.

I write well. I speak well. I am persuasive in my communications with peers, superiors, and clients. I am able to learn languages quickly, and retain the ability while dormant.

I am warm and full of empathy, but lack emotional engagement in business. People like me. I am able to see the best in everyone and still recognize the warning signs of dishonesty, insecurity, and imperfect intentions. I am very loyal to those who earn my loyalty.

Still, I am not patient. I like to move quickly, sometimes more quickly than is prudent. In my haste, I am prone to forget or disregard protocol. In my haste, I might not communicate as completely as I should.

I am a perfectionist. I am overly self-critical and often demand more of myself than is possible. I expect nearly as much of others as of myself. I am outspoken and quick to speak, even when a period of calm or silence would best resolve the situation.

I have difficulty working for someone whom I don't respect, or for a cause in which I don't believe. I will not lie or fib to please others, and instead sometimes air my opinions when silent agreement would expedite the accomplishment of the task at hand.

Finally, I have gaps in my business training and business skills. In investment banking and private equity I have employed financial analysis skills, and yet my understanding is incomplete due to limited financial coursework. I have on-the-job experience, but have not undergone a training program or classical academic business training. I have built up industry understanding in wireless software and a few other areas, but I do not have in-depth knowledge of most areas of business or the broad perspective gained by study of a comprehensive business curriculum.

ANALYSIS

Elizabeth's essay is a fantastic illustration of how to convey personality and credibility. Its unique stream-of-consciousness style makes it stand out. The author takes a risk by not including an introduction or a conclusion, but the choice of style amplifies her character. The seemingly endless list of specific traits and characteristics flows from one sentence to the next, building the reader's anticipation for more. While other essays may focus on a handful of strengths and weaknesses, Elizabeth's barrage of bite-sized details provides an unusual degree of breadth without a shadow of conceit. The writing style reflects her personality; it is representative of the eloquent but impatient, and ultimately very self-aware author.

The discussion of weaknesses is as detailed and specific as that of strengths. However, Elizabeth manages to imply that addressing them is highly relevant to her professional life. The

VII. Strengths and Weaknesses

concluding need to undergo formal business training leaves a clear impression. Without stating so outright, Elizabeth makes it obvious that attending HBS would be a major step in her personal development.

BARTEK TRZEBINSKI

I explored my character and confronted perceptions of myself with reality by asking closest friends about my strengths and weaknesses. They uniformly mentioned maturity, ambition, and logical thinking as my greatest assets. These characteristics have been reflected in my strategic approach to life. Since high school, I have thought five or ten years forward, set challenging goals and persistently achieved them. For instance, I managed a Boy Scout unit not just because it was fun and gave me satisfaction, but also because it gave me leadership practice early in my career. I learned foreign languages in anticipation of international assignments and eventual opening of the Polish marketplace. I also established an investment fund to gain hands-on experience in investing. Privately, I particularly pride myself in the ability to connect and work effectively with people from various backgrounds and cultures, be it top managers, politicians or artists. I successfully coached inner-city youth at a summer camp in Poland. I have worked in offices in Europe, Asia, and the U.S., and I was equally professional in each environment due to my flexibility and eagerness to learn about new cultures. I have always taken care to maintain and develop personal relationships. Despite recent extensive business travels, I have stayed in touch with my friends and colleagues.

On the other hand, I wish I were more willing to take risks. This feature may be a derivative of my recent position as acting project risk manager, where I was responsible for recognizing and evaluating all potential risk areas in project-financed transactions. I recognize that risk aversion was advantageous in my risk management job. However, at this early stage in my career and life, I believe I should be more of a risk-taker to benefit from my still steep learning curve, while experiencing new processes and practices. Therefore, I intend to continually take new challenges in business, which is reflected in my plans to eventually establish business incubators and/or a foundation in Poland. In stressful situations, I tend to be overly critical and demanding of myself and others. My exactness may be fastidious to subordinates and colleagues, so I strive to "loosen up" and be more patient without sacrificing the quality of work. I am working on being able to identify the optimal level of meticulousness in each task, and to motivate others to do their best under tense circumstances.

ANALYSIS

Honesty and credibility are the irrefutable strengths of this essay. In the first paragraph, Bartek sets himself apart by sharing the extent of his self-exploration effort. Not only did he look inward to understand his strengths and weaknesses, but also asked his closest friends for input. This demonstrates that he is not only self-aware, but open to constructive criticism from others. His strengths are deeply rooted elements of his character that have evolved from childhood, and he uses a series of detailed examples to illustrate how they impact every area of his life.

Bartek manages to divulge a large number of details about his life experiences and personality while ensuring that they all reinforce one another. Each word and example in this well-crafted essay lends credibility to his strengths and weaknesses. Because the reader gains a strong sense of Bartek's character after reading

VII. Strengths and Weaknesses

the first paragraph, it is easy to understand why his weaknesses are true weaknesses and not disguised strengths. For example, his reluctance to take risks is in line with his strength of being a careful forward planner. He uses an anecdote to support this weakness and details the steps he has taken to overcome it. It is difficult to question such a frank self-assessment.

Isa Wegner

I think that enthusiastic, professional, and international, with all the positive and negative implications, would be a good way to summarize my strengths and weaknesses. When I decide to take something on, whether in business or in personal life, I tend to be very enthusiastic about it: I want to give it my best, get as much as possible out of it, and enjoy myself while doing so. I put my heart into everything I do. Therefore, enthusiasm is one of my biggest strengths: it makes it easy for me to get on with anyone, to motivate people, and to create a fun and supportive environment around me. My positive nature has also helped me to get through tough times (whether on projects or during difficult company situations). However, enthusiasm is also one of my weaknesses by making me relatively impatient with people that have a negative or cynical outlook. Because I fully engage in anything I do, a cynical attitude goes against what I stand for and believe in. Therefore, I find it more emotionally challenging to deal with people who have a more neutral attitude towards their work.

I would also describe myself as professional. When I take on a task, I want to do it to the best of my ability and make no compromises. I find it crucially important to be respectful among colleagues and towards superiors and clients, especially in today's sometimes very casual workplace. Professionalism makes me a thorough and appreciated colleague, who provides robust and well-considered analyses and conclusions. However, this very thoroughness and perfectionism sometimes prevents me from taking on tasks that I feel I have too little experience in. Although I am always ready to take on challenges when I have the right support mechanism, I never make bullish statements about my abilities unless I am convinced I am well prepared to do the job, sometimes leading me to underestimate my abilities.

Finally, being international is also both a strength and a weakness. Having traveled a lot during my studies and my work has given me a lot of confidence of being able to stand on my own, even in a foreign environment. I cherish international contact. On the downside, being very international has left me less deeply rooted in any one place than people who have spent their entire lives in the same community.

ANALYSIS

Isa's essay takes an unusual but effective approach by equating her three strengths with her three weaknesses. A simple declaration that a strength taken to an extreme can become a weakness could be viewed as vague and abstract. In this case, it is the specific and detailed explanations that make the essay successful. Isa provides three specific and personal instances to illustrate her point. Thus, in addition to describing her strengths and weaknesses, she also demonstrates a high degree of self-awareness, maturity, and balance in her life.

Departing from the standard response format to an essay topic is always a little risky. Taking too many liberties can render the essay ineffective in addressing the core question. If successful, on the other hand, it can make an essay stand out.

Raul Almeida Cadena

I believe a person's strengths are reflected in their accomplishments and in the path they have followed from where they began in life to where they have arrived.

I think adaptability and flexibility are important strengths I developed. I grew up in a rather humble family and following work forced us to move all around Brazil. I was born in the poor northeast of Brazil, lived in the far north and spent my adolescence in the developed southeast. Befriending people from various economic and social backgrounds and always being ready to pack up and leave has forced me to develop a great deal of flexibility, making me ready to face adversity and change, to adapt to ever-changing situations and to deal with various cultures and values.

Another important strength that I believe my achievements reflect is determination. Throughout my life, I have had rewarding experiences, such as when I was an intern at Exxon during my senior year in college. The company was located sixty miles away and every Thursday I had to wake up at 4:30 A.M. and take three different bus rides before making it to Exxon in order to start working at 8:00 A.M. After working all day and spending the night in a youth hostel, I would repeat the drudgery on Friday and only make it back home at 11:00 at night. All of this while facing a tough curriculum in the most demanding engineering school in the country. The experience taught me the value of effort and commitment, not to mention it boosted my confidence when it came to facing the challenges the future held.

My main weakness is that I still focus too much on details. At a consulting company, learning to apply the "80/20" rule is critical to a successful project leader. By focusing on details, I end up misplacing my efforts and spending valuable time on details that will not add to my intuition and judgment. Although such ability comes with experience, I think two years of real-life case discussions at Harvard can guarantee the development of such qualities while shortening the time it would take should I wait to simply attain them on my own.

Another weakness that I have been working on a lot is assertiveness. I still need to be more effective in defending ideas and getting my point across in the presence of senior management. Although I feel I have improved a lot since I first joined BCG as an untried engineer, I am conscious that I still have a ways to go in order to get where I want.

ANALYSIS

Raul's essay is a great demonstration of how to convey sincerity and ambition. He uses the first two paragraphs to reveal that his strengths are unique because of his humble beginnings. By illustrating that his path from childhood to BCG was not a smoothly paved road, the reader gains a sense of the magnitude of his personal and professional development. Through his straightforward and illustrative writing style, Raul makes it easy to visualize his life experiences.

He does not attempt to elicit the reader's sympathy, but rather sincerely shares what it felt like to be from a humble family, to move around as a child, and to travel for several hours to his internship during college. These vignettes bring his strengths to life and simultaneously serve to highlight Raul's diverse experiences. His casual and sincere tone is indicative of a friendly and engaging personality, while the essay overall makes it clear that he is hardworking, ambitious, and successful.

Raul names two specific weaknesses. These are areas for personal development that have arisen in the context of his consulting work, but serve to indicate a genuine sense of self-awareness. Cleverly, Raul shows how attending HBS would be instrumental in addressing these areas for improvement. His weaknesses actually strengthen his case as an applicant!

TAMARA NALL

Two of my greatest strengths are (1) my ability to grasp the "big picture" and (2) my initiative—particularly in adding value to the institutions or environments in which I have interacted. I always scrutinize an opportunity to determine if other possibilities exist and if there is a way to grow the opportunity past its current level.

For example, I trained a government client on a financial and operational model that I had developed. During these sessions, I seized the opportunity to listen to the client's needs outside of the project's scope. In fact, one of the senior executives was so impressed with the quality of work and my genuine concern that she wanted to allocate her extra budget to another project for Booz Allen to further improve the client's operations. I took the idea to a principal and, as a result, my initiative led to work extensions for the firm.

My holistic, entrepreneurial perspective also extended to the community. In New York and Atlanta, I have organized several clothing and food drives for South Africa and Ghana and have sought individuals and groups to join these efforts. What was the big picture? For some, these drives represented the first opportunity to become involved in a foreign community service-project and thus introduced them to a simple way to give back.

My greatest weakness is my emotional involvement with my work. Oftentimes, clients expect recommendations, based on sound analysis, regardless of the implications. For one client, my team and I had to offer analytically driven recommendations to a client based on a congressional mandate. However, based on client interviews, I knew that many of these client members were not ready to assume some of the responsibilities inherent in our recommendations. Therefore, I struggled with my expectation that they would have to learn how to "walk before they crawled." On my current project, I am working on a post-merger integration project of two agribusiness clients. This is my first project in which possible layoffs and plant closings, due to excess workforces, may be an issue. Ever since our initial discussion of these options, I have had difficulty responding to the likelihood of people losing their jobs. At times, I have had to remind myself that my job involves providing objective recommendations without any emotional involvement. Otherwise, my emotion may cloud my judgment. However, I am aggressively thinking of ways to care for the client and also provide logical, sound business solutions. With counsel and experience, though, I am finding the true balance between my emotions and business acuity.

ANALYSIS

Tamara's essay is effective because she conveys two of her strengths through two descriptive anecdotes. She illustrates well how these characteristics come together in both her personal and professional life. In addition, she uses examples that have the added benefit of implicitly highlighting several additional strengths, such as her ability to communicate effectively, work one-on-one with senior-level management, and lead large groups in pursuit of a common purpose. Through these examples, Tamara comes across as a well-rounded individual.

Half of Tamara's essay is devoted to two examples of her greatest weakness: her emotional involvement in her work. The self-critique is effective because Tamara is honest and specific

VII. Strengths and Weaknesses

about how this aspect of her personality has impacted her work. Her maturity and forethought are conveyed in her awareness of how this weakness is likely to affect her in the future. Tamara's point about seeking counsel in this area to find the appropriate balance is key in connecting the weakness to goals for improvement.

Anonymous

My main strengths include being both academically able and intellectually curious. I have proved myself to be as strong in economics as I am in English literature, mirrored in my work by an ability to read statistics and scripts with equal ease. In study, not only can I master the finer points of perfect competition and postcolonial literature, but I also come alive around these subjects. In the classroom at the London School of Economics, I argue with more passion, compassion, and insight than the aggregate of all my classmates.

In the real world, filming on the streets of the Bronx, I developed a skill base far removed from the one I had acquired within the ivory towers of academia. I was able to adapt instantly to ever-changing, challenging, and sometimes hostile situations. These circumstances facilitated my development into a strong leader who could guide others under the most testing circumstances. Working with film crews comprised of a hundred people—from the director to the driver—also taught me how to operate effectively as part of an incredibly diverse team.

Survival in a competitive freelance environment depends not only on how well you do, but also on how well you relate to people. I am simultaneously able to accomplish results and develop lasting working relationships. I communicate very clearly and problem-solve quickly and objectively. Through these strengths I have developed into a skilled negotiator and I am increasingly working in a deal-making capacity.

I am prepared to take risks and embrace new challenges; in choosing to work in film I took an uncertain course and, in the spirit of entrepreneurship, set up a company in a foreign country. I possess an extremely broad worldview; I have traveled and worked in many different environments and through the arts and my MBA I seek to further expand my outlook.

As in many cases, my flaws are bound up in my virtues. I am extremely determined, and if I set myself a course of action I will follow it to the very end. However, underlying this is a difficulty to stop fighting for an outcome which does not merit the time and energy invested in it. In teamwork situations I can find it difficult to engage with those who do not share my enthusiasm and commitment to a project. I can sometimes be tactless when conveying my opinions but with time I am learning to be more sensitive.

ANALYSIS

Simply creating a list of strengths would not make for an effective essay. The author, however, uses specific experiences to cleverly paint a picture of herself as an effective and dynamic leader. Aware that academic excellence alone is insufficient for being a good manager, the author demonstrates her more pragmatic business strengths: flexibility, problem-solving, and communication.

The essay leaves a lasting impression of a self-aware woman who studied economics and literature, honed her leadership skills through film and took a risk by starting a company in a foreign country. The diversity of her experience makes her an interesting candidate for HBS, while her understanding of how to apply her strengths in different environments illustrates a high level of managerial savvy.

The final paragraph addressing weaknesses seems a little brief, especially given the amount of space the author devotes to her

VII. Strengths and Weaknesses

strengths. Nonetheless, the author is quite specific about her major areas for personal development. There is no attempt to position them as strengths, and she is quite firm in her commitment to improve over time. Such a matter-of-fact treatment is probably just another facet of her pragmatic, goal-oriented character.

Francisco Sousa Pimentel

In order to better convey who I am, I would like to detail three strong character traits that I believe stand out in my personality: *initiative*, *maturity*, and *open-mindedness*. There are also two areas—*communications* and *attention to detail*—which I have had the opportunity to improve over the past years. My challenge going forward is to improve my communications skills and to be more detailed without compromising the pace of my initiative or the drive to get things done.

People who know me tend to point out my *intellectual curiosity* and *initiative* as my most distinctive traits. These characteristics are the result of the environment where I was brought up, where commitment to hard work and ideals were considered key to achieve success. I have incorporated these thoughts and became eager to implement the ideas I found important.

Maturity is another strong element of my personality. However, this essential ingredient of a decision-maker did not come easily for me. Two years before completing high school, my parents got divorced and, as the oldest of four children, I often had to step into a parental role. This was probably the most difficult phase of my life. I came out of those times more responsible, mature in judgment, and more certain of what I wanted.

The other fundamental trait of my personality is my *open-mindedness*. I have always been very tolerant toward other cultures and interested in understanding different perspectives. That is why I have traveled a lot and tried to get to know different people from different cultures. While at university, I applied to spend a full year in Barcelona in an exchange program. It was one of the best years of my life. I also decided to visit Eastern European countries and Russia, be in places like Auschwitz or experience the liberal atmosphere of the Netherlands. I believe this transformed me into a more autonomous thinker and conscious person.

The last two years at McKinsey have helped me overcome some of my weaknesses, like *oral communication* and *attention to detail*. I actually only became aware of these limitations as I had to convey my messages to senior executives. I realized I had trouble tailoring the message to the audience, as well as summing up messages with complex and serious implications. I also recognized that my drive led me to sometimes overlook detail, which is essential to ensure the full accuracy of the content. Fortunately, I have had exposure to great mentors and plenty of opportunities to work on these aspects. Feedback that I have received shows me that I have made tangible progress.

ANALYSIS

Francisco uses the strengths part of this essay to explain why he would do well at HBS. He is a hard-working, mature, and open-minded individual and, it is logical to conclude, someone who would seem to thrive in a diverse place like HBS. The weaknesses section is honest but a little risky. Few applicants, for example, are likely to admit difficulties with oral communication. That is not to say all applicants to HBS are actually good at it (because many are not when they arrive on campus). Francisco's weakness is a risk, though, because Harvard's case method demands a certain comfort level with putting forward and defending arguments in front a group of people who may have differing points of view. To suggest you are not good at doing that is to say that you may not be compatible with a core aspect of the HBS experience. The counterargument of course, is that someone like Francisco should come to HBS precisely because he would benefit the most by being there (given the school's emphasis on speaking publicly). Because Francisco was a successful candidate the lesson here is that it rarely hurts to be honest.

The end of the essay would be more satisfying if Francisco included a concrete example of how he has overcome his weaknesses. For example, a story about a successful presentation to a hostile client would be more meaningful than vaguely saying that "feedback" shows he has made progress. Whenever possible, be specific. Do not just say you improved; instead, come up with an example of how you did. Your essay will come across as more genuine if you can do that. In this case, since Francisco is especially open about his weaknesses, there is very little risk that anyone would think he is not being candid. The only criticism, really, is that we want to know more.

VIII. WHY DO YOU NEED AN HBS MBA?

Why do you wish to pursue an MBA degree from Harvard Business School? What are your career aspirations and why?

What are your career aspirations, and how can Harvard Business School help you to reach them?

You have answered all the other questions brilliantly, but do you know what you want to be when you grow up? Have you scoped a long-term vision for your career? Do you truly need an MBA *now*? And why from HBS?

This seemingly straightforward question may be the most important one on the application. It can also be the most challenging. You think you know the answers. Or you know you should know the answers. But when you sit down to write, you find yourself struggling to clearly express your career plans and how an MBA fits into the whole picture. Initial struggles do not mean that you are not ready for an MBA or that you are not a fabulous candidate for Harvard Business School. This question reaches to the core of who you are and what you want to accomplish in life—difficult issues to resolve and articulate.

To start off, make sure that you understand your personal vision—how you want to shape yourself and the world around you. Questions to think through to help craft your vision include: What brings me happiness? What are my strengths and weaknesses? What are my most important values? Writing the other five application essays first should help focus your thinking. Being able to define what drives you as a person is the cornerstone of a successful essay on this subject. Otherwise, the prose will come out sounding canned and dispassionate.

Try to structure your thinking—but not necessarily your essay—by using the following steps:

First, put your current and past experience in context, particularly establishing how it is relevant to your future goals. Second, define your short-term and long-term career plans. These should be realistic and based on your experience and personal interests. Think about the impact you want to have on the world and then break it down into stages of how you will achieve it. Third, assess the gaps in your experience and education and identify how an MBA program will fill those holes. Finally, decide what makes the specifics of Harvard Business School appropriate to your goals and connect your career ambitions to the mission of the school. Then think about what *you* can contribute to the MBA program.

The essays in this chapter include all or most of the elements mentioned. And although not explicitly stated, they all convey a consistent sense of personal vision linked to career ambitions. While the style and content vary dramatically, all of these essays explore career paths that will ultimately satisfy the writers' personal ambitions to be an agent of change and lay out how HBS will serve as a transforming experience to aid them in attaining their goals.

—Sara Cherlin

Terese Molina

Throughout my professional career, I have experienced the mergers and acquisitions process from a number of different perspectives—investment banking, private equity, incubator/accelerator, and real estate management. Each of these opportunities has enabled me to build upon my transactional skills and develop a strong financial background. After almost six years of deal-related experience in various industries I have decided to pursue a career in private equity, with the ultimate goal of becoming a managing partner at a private equity fund. My past work experiences have prepared me with the practical know-how and quantitative skills to prosper in this field. Nonetheless, I must gain more exposure to marketing and strategic management issues in order to accomplish my short- and long-term career goals.

An MBA education from the Harvard Business School will provide me with superior management skills and a greater level of business sophistication. Harvard's innovative curriculum, as well as its emphasis on entrepreneurship and the case method, will expose me to the intricacies of negotiation as well as entrepreneurial and strategic management. By working with a diverse group of professionals in study groups and team projects, I will become familiar with foreign business practices and techniques. The lively discussions and seminars given by CEOs of *Fortune* 500 companies will introduce me to the personal qualities inherent in an outstanding senior-level manager. In my future career as a managing partner of a private equity fund, I will, undoubtedly, hold several board positions in portfolio companies, so a solid background in corporate strategy will be essential to my professional goals.

Clearly, a Harvard MBA education will offer me the analytical skills, the teamwork and leadership instincts, and the business savvy to succeed in the private equity sector. At HBS, I will mature into a well-rounded business professional, building long-lasting relationships with my colleagues and taking advantage of Harvard's exceptional business resources.

ANALYSIS

This is a tight, well-structured essay that clearly lays out what the applicant hopes to learn by going to HBS. Terese is specific about what she wants to do after business school (rise to become a managing partner at a private equity fund) and what she needs to learn to get there (marketing and corporate strategy). Terese also does a nice job highlighting what is perhaps the most critical task for a private equity manager: evaluating CEOs and senior-level managers of portfolio companies. She makes the case that by being at HBS she will meet these future leaders and learn what drives them and makes them successful. The only area this essay misses the mark is that Terese could highlight what she brings to HBS and how she would contribute to the community. In such a short format you have to pick and chose what you include, but a sentence or two in this regard would have shed further light on what kind of person Terese is. It is a small criticism of an otherwise solid essay.

ANONYMOUS

My long-term goal is to be a leader in the energy business of a diversified resources company such as Rio Tinto, because such a position would enable me to make a positive contribution to some of the important challenges—global consolidation, for example—facing the resource industry.

While my operational experience will be invaluable in achieving this goal, I require specific skills that will not be acquired on mine sites. Instead, formal training in finance, general management, and international business will be required. HBS courses such as Leading Change and Organizational Renewal and Managing International Trade and Investment will provide these skills.

HBS is the best environment in which to acquire these skills for three reasons:

Working on real business problems as an analyst taught me a great deal about business in general. This indicates that the case-study method used by Harvard would be an extremely effective way to acquire the mind-set necessary to achieve my career goals.

Addressing the challenges faced by the resource industry effectively will require empathy with decision-makers in a wide range of roles—financial, regulatory, customers, and competitors. Working closely with other students—given their diverse interests and experiences—would help me develop this empathy. At the same time, I feel my unusual professional experiences and interests would be a valuable contribution to the HBS community.

The problems faced by the resource industry require a global view. The global focus of HBS's curriculum, and the broad backgrounds of its students, would provide an excellent environment in which to meet this requirement.

After graduation, I intend to join the business development group of a diversified resources company. In such a role, a global view is crucial in identifying the commercial opportunities available in the resource industry, and to assess the implications of those opportunities. The specific skills acquired at HBS would allow me to maximize the value of those opportunities.

ANALYSIS

The author is very specific about what he hopes to do after HBS and why continuing to work is not an option (a mine would not expose him to finance or general management training, for example). It is often helpful to make the case why not going to business school is not an option. In this case, the author does this quite well.

Beyond that, the strength of this essay lies in the author's deep understanding of HBS. He clearly has done his homework and comes across as intimately familiar with the dynamics of class discussions. He also recognizes, and is right to point out, that given his atypical background he would contribute just as much to HBS as he would gain from being there. Never hesitate to mention what you would bring to the school. This is not to say you should boast; however, you do need to make a convincing argument about how HBS would be better off by having you there. In this particular essay, the author could have gone even a step further in describing what he brings to the table by providing additional specifics of his "unusual professional experiences and interests."

Rayford Lee Davis

By working in the consumer goods, retail, and e-tail practices at McKinsey, I explored the option of turning a childhood love for branded products into a full-blown career. Moving to Ethcentric, I dug deeper into these prospects and began to focus on how companies connect with their consumers through target marketing. From these experiences, I've learned that companies create products that reflect their perspectives of consumers' everyday lives, while people purchase specific products to exhibit their own view of their lifestyles. Combining this insight with my professional and personal experiences, I realize my professional goal is to create a global branded products company that will improve the self-images of ethnic communities by promoting the most wonderful aspects of each culture in its product marketing.

To do this, I'll need the most rigorous general management training applicable across multiple platforms, the strongest network to leverage as my business develops and the most renowned credentials for the capital markets. First, Harvard's unique case method approach will elevate my ability to make sound decisions with limited information. My diverse professional experiences in research and development, plant operations, retail operations, mergers and acquisitions, interactive marketing, and grassroots campaigning have taught me that complete information never exists. Secondly, the HBS experience will provide me with a global network of leaders on which to call as my business grows from a regional start-up to a national conglomerate to an international vehicle for cultural appreciation. By taking leadership roles in the African-American

Student Union, the most influential African-American alumni network in the world, and the Retail and Apparel Club, a rare gem exclusive to HBS among top general management programs, I will develop lasting relationships with world leaders. Finally, I will need to raise capital to grow this business. The credibility gained with a Harvard MBA will drive discussions with potential investors quickly beyond my management capabilities to the execution of my ideas.

As I consider the tools I need to achieve my professional goals, the Harvard Business School is the only place for me to get them all. I can't wait to start!

ANALYSIS

Rayford's essay clearly depicts how an MBA from Harvard Business School would help him achieve his goals and conveys bubbling enthusiasm for it. He starts out by providing the context of his relevant past experience and then cleanly segues into how it has led to his long-term career goals. His desire to work on consumer products is realistic based on his past experience in consumer goods and retail. Additionally, his commitment to the ethnic communities appears genuine as demonstrated in further comments about becoming actively involved in the African-American Student Union.

By citing this and other student clubs, Rayford makes a strong case for why the HBS program is specifically suited for him and how he plans to assume leadership on campus. While some of the other comments about the case method and strong network are not boldly original, they do not have to be; they still show that Rayford has thought through which particular characteristics make the program appealing to him. All of these aspects are clearly tied to his career goals of starting a business. Overall, Rayford shows clear direction and purpose based on experience and planning. The exclamatory statement at the end works within the tone of his essay and conveys genuine enthusiasm.

IMAN TYSON

My career aspirations are twofold:

First, become president of a Ford subsidiary in South America (i.e., Ford Argentina, Chile or Venezuela).

Second, increase the awareness of the benefits of diversity and socioeconomic development in the South American corporate sector by:

- Becoming a board member of a consultancy group that helps corporations leverage their internal diversity, develop effective corporate citizenship strategies, and find creative means to develop successful paradigms for corporate and social interaction.

- Establishing a continental award and grant program, funded by corporations, which recognizes individual, group, and corporate achievements to socioeconomic development.

Having gained leadership experiences in product development and operations across four continents and with a need for a strong foundation of general business skills, the HBS MBA becomes the *essential* stepping-stone to my career aspirations.

HBS will help me achieve my aspirations in the following ways:

Global problem-solving

I believe the HBS MBA will give me the skills and leadership thinking necessary to make the best decisions to resolve complex global problems. Through the HBS Latin American Research Center in Buenos Aires, I hope to conduct research with the objective of developing a corporate strategy designed to increase profit and improve social conditions, as well as improve my business Spanish.

Dynamic learning

After observing a study group and three HBS classes, I experienced a unique learning atmosphere of insight, diversity, and perspective and an atmosphere most compatible with my learning style. The interactive classroom participation, cold calls, and the case study learning method will give me the unique opportunity to engage, contribute, challenge, and be challenged by the perspectives and backgrounds of my classmates and faculty.

International credibility and a global network

The global reputation of HBS will be a critical vote of confidence that will ensure key international opportunities at levels where I can make an immediate impact and maintain my career path. Also, with the vast network of overseas HBS alumni, I will be able call upon skills, influence, and leadership to refine my vision, build corporate alliances, and establish friendships.

VIII. Why Do You Need an HBS MBA?

The total experience

My discussions with alumni have convinced me that HBS will give me an invaluable experience of learning, relationships, and enjoyment. This transforming experience will help me forge the character, courage, and confidence necessary to reach my professional and personal goals.

ANALYSIS

Iman's essay veers away from the traditional multi-paragraph format to assume the style of a business memo, showing that alternative structures can be equally powerful. Iman poignantly illustrates how the HBS program will guide him to his specific career goals. The message is very consistent throughout the essay and is generously supported with well-documented details about HBS. Iman has obviously done his homework and shows great interest in the curriculum and the broader benefits of an HBS education. Like some of the preceding essays, this one could have benefited from at least a few words addressing what Iman will bring to HBS. The very detailed list of benefits he expects to derive from attending could have been nicely balanced with a corresponding list of his contributions to the school and the learning environment.

MONISHA KAPILA

My career aspiration is to be a leader in economic development, particularly international economic development. I believe the best way to achieve a sustainable change in poverty is to create business opportunities and jobs in poor areas. Short term, I plan to work for organizations such as the United Nations, the World Bank, and foundations that influence growth in developing countries. In the long run, I plan to lead an international organization that helps countries identify their competitive advantages for business and sustainable development.

Through my past work experience, I have gained tremendous business skills and understanding of economic development theories. In my current role at ICIC, I am applying Professor Michael Porter's theories to help inner-city areas identify competitive advantages to attract businesses and create jobs for their residents. I would like to broaden the application of this economic development model to developing countries around the world. To do this successfully, I need to learn more about business strategy and how to manage large organizations, both core components of Harvard's MBA program.

Pursuing a degree from HBS will provide me the platform I need to achieve my career aspirations. In particular, the general management focus, the case method, and the Social Enterprise Initiative will prepare me to be an effective leader in economic development. First, the general management focus will provide me with the breadth of skills that I will need to lead and run an organization. Second, the case method will prepare me to deal with the challenges faced by leaders in making decisions with limited information. Finally, the classes and programs available through the Social Enterprise Initiative will help me learn to lead in the social sector. Outside of the classroom, I plan to take a leadership role in organizations such as the Social Enterprise Club and the International Development Club so that I can network with students and faculty who share my interests.

I have visited HBS classes and was impressed by the diverse perspectives and the engaging discussions. I believe I will be an asset at HBS because I will contribute my passion for leveraging business in economic development, my experience in the for-profit and non-profit sectors, and my initiative both inside and outside the classroom. I look forward to being at HBS next year and am certain that I will be a valuable member of the community.

ANALYSIS

Monisha does an impressive job of touching on all the key elements that this question is asking for, and she does so in a poignant and well-written way. The first sentence provides a guiding "mission" to her career aspirations, followed by specific short- and long-term goals that appear realistic based on her background and interests. She also names specific organizations, lending credibility to the thoughtfulness of her plan.

She also is able to clearly demonstrate *why* she needs an MBA and why she needs it *now*. Monisha wants to broaden her knowledge around an area in which she has already achieved some expertise (economic development) in order to transition from a domestic-oriented position to one global in scope. She understands the finer points of the HBS program and links them to her career goals.

VIII. Why Do You Need an HBS MBA?

Monisha exhibits commitment to the program by referring to her HBS class visit and indicating her interest in the discussion. She takes the question one step further by showing not only how the program will benefit her, but how she can in turn enrich the HBS community and add to the learning environment. The essay is persuasive and ultimately a compelling case to admit Monisha to HBS.

Reina Mizuno

My immediate goal after getting an MBA is to continue working for a global consulting firm and to help foreign companies enter and excel in the Japanese market. Although most of the major American corporations have entered and built their presences in Japan a long time ago, there are many small- and medium-sized American companies who have no idea about their potential in the Japanese market or any international market. Yet there are few resources in Japan with enough industry expertise, communication skills, international network, and management skills to help. This is where I want to contribute.

To attain the most flexibility in multinational consulting, my long-term goal is to take over my father's business and expand it to offer more services. About fifteen years ago, my father launched CoTech International, Inc., which files and settles international intellectual property cases and runs a search database for Madrid Protocol, an international trademark protocol. I would like to combine the company's current service of intellectual property transactions and research with a consulting service to help clients enter foreign markets.

I am impressed with HBS's focus on developing global business leaders, analyzing successful businesses through case studies, and building an international student body. An HBS education will offer me an objective view of the characteristics of a successful business, by learning different cases of multinational businesses in an academic environment with a world-class faculty and state-of-the-art facilities. At the same time, I believe that my bicultural-bilingual background and experiences would be a great contribution to the school in creating an interesting and international student body. It may be too late to be a pioneer for large businesses in Japan, but with an HBS education under my belt, I can become a Japanese pioneer in expanding international business opportunities for small businesses.

ANALYSIS

Reina's essay is extraordinarily clear and concise. She lays out her short- and long-term goals in two well-written paragraphs, substantiating her case with clear evidence of how she will go about achieving them. Her goals seem a realistic progression of what will be reasonably within her reach right after business school as well as how she will expand the scope through her father's business. Reina's commitment to helping small business grow in Japan is consistently woven throughout the essay and to her concluding remarks; the consistency adds to the essay's sincerity. She states clear reasons for wanting to pursue an MBA at Harvard and trumps the question by emphasizing why she would be a healthy addition to the HBS student body.

GREGORY THOMPSON

"Harvard Business School? Are you kidding? It's too competitive! You're too young! Continue with your career. In two more years, you'll be making plenty of money." That is the reaction from my colleagues and friends when I tell them I am applying to business school.

Despite resistance from my peers, my desire to attend HBS could not be stronger. My short-term goal is to become a financial manager in the nonprofit sector with my long-term goal to found and lead my own foundation focused on inner-city development. Through my volunteer activities with St. Jude Children's Research Hospital, Habitat for Humanity, and Hands on Memphis, I have recognized a strong need for business managers in the nonprofit sector. After attending HBS, I aspire to lead an organization that addresses the needs of underprivileged citizens in my community. Earning an MBA at this point in my life is a perfect choice, providing me with an opportunity to acquire the tools I need to begin a new chapter.

So what have I been up to in my career that has led to this realization? Quite surprisingly, I have been working as an investment banker for Morgan Keegan in what has been coined the "world of higher finance." Indeed, like many young, ambitious college graduates, I have been chasing the golden dream—BMW, limousines, three-story house, first-class service. Here we come, guns blazing! What is happening to me now? Did I suddenly develop a conscience, or did too many late nights at the office make me delusional and idealistic? No, I believe something else is at work. I have finally had the courage to pursue what truly makes me happy, ignoring what is going to make me the most money or what my friends might think.

"But why nonprofit?" my coworkers jeer. "Are you going to be a social worker or go to Africa and live in a hut?" Absolutely not, my fiancée would kill me. But there are incredible opportunities to become part of social-enterprise initiatives at U.S. corporations or manage independent nonprofits. Historically, nonprofits have lacked savvy business managers. These entities need talented MBA graduates to help find creative solutions to challenges in the community. Harvard's social-enterprise program will enable me to explore issues in nonprofit management and to expand my business skills while providing me access to professional opportunities after graduation.

Community service has been a passionate part of my life, from my experiences mentoring at the Boys & Girls Club of Knoxville to my more recent involvement with Habitat for Humanity and Hands on Memphis. Through these leadership experiences, I have found something special in my life that I want to make an integral part of my career.

The case study method at HBS will be an invaluable opportunity to interact with students that have the same aspirations as I do. The diversity of the student body will enable me to see the world through different eyes, to broaden my perspective on how to approach different problems and to build a network of friendships that will last a lifetime. Through these types of experiences, I am confident I will make a meaningful impact on a nonprofit organization postgraduation.

ANALYSIS

The candor and conversational tone set Greg's essay apart. He distinctly states his short-term and long-term goals in the nonprofit sector and generously supports his career-switching objective with evidence of his personal devotion to the community. HBS prides itself on being a transformational experience, and Greg illustrates how he is boldly going to take advantage of this.

Most importantly, he is able to make a clear case for why an MBA is so important to him now, at a point where he has finally mustered the courage to weigh his personal ambitions against the "practical banker's path" he has followed. While the banking lifestyle might be appropriate for others, Greg realizes it is clearly not the right one for him. To make the change, an HBS education including exposure to nonprofit management through the social enterprise program he mentions will be invaluable.

Greg's writing style allows the reader to experience the soul-searching he has gone through to reach this moment of career clarity. He is frank not only about his career epiphany, but also about the limitations he expects to encounter. This forthrightness validates the sincerity of his plans.

ANNE MORRISS

I have watched the world change around people who were unprepared for its transformation. I have defined *commodity* for Brazilian coffee brokers whose market suddenly seemed to ignore them. I have argued about Mercosur with a tired finance minister in Ecuador, and have seen Dominican friends fight for jobs in a new *zona franca* condemned by international labor groups.

I want to help clarify the confusion, and I want the Harvard Business School to be my accomplice.

I am choosing HBS for the traditional outputs. I want to increase my impact on organizations, to join a network of people with the courage to reach difficult goals, to gain unmatched credibility as a messenger. HBS has an outstanding reputation for offering these things, and my research confirms it. Most of the HBS students and alumni I know are risking their definitions of greatness.

I also want the journey. I want the daily luxury of exploring the world with the extraordinary community that HBS builds. I want to engage Frances Frei on my company's failed technology dream and see Haitian competitiveness from Michael Porter's perspective. I want to argue with James Austin about the private sector's ability to drive social change and discuss the responsibilities of corporations with exceptional peers who will translate their convictions into meaningful action.

I came to ontheFRONTIER to learn to fight poverty in a new global context. I want to advance that fight, and I want to test and improve my strategy at HBS, a place that will hold me to the highest standards of analysis and tutor me in the messy art of leadership.

ANALYSIS

This poetic essay grabs your attention from the get-go. It snubs the traditional thesis-plus-evidence structure and craftily spins the rationale for pursuing an MBA at HBS. Most striking still is the passion that Anne exudes for impacting the world around her.

While not stated outright, and even without the context of the entire application, the reader can deduce Anne's ambitions to continue in her field of economic development. She describes her past experience through expressive snippets of her work in emerging markets. These accounts are ever more powerful because of the personal touches she colors them with—a conversation with Ecuador's finance minister, friends seeking employment in the Dominican Republic. And despite all these global accomplishments, she makes a strong case for returning to school for an MBA.

Anne provides incisive examples of why HBS is her school of choice. She has obviously done background research and is familiar with the faculty and their work. In the process, she exposes her own personal interests and motivations. The strength of this essay lies both in the nobility of Anne's goals and in the eloquence of the delivery. The reader is convinced through Anne's well-expressed convictions that she will be a powerful agent of change.

IX. OPTIONAL ESSAY

Is there any other information that you believe would be helpful to the board in understanding you better and in considering your application? Please be concise.

If you are like most applicants, you are probably wondering whether the "optional essay" is really optional. What if all the other candidates include one and you do not? Then again, after six other essays, what else can you write about?

The whole point of the essay set is to express as many aspects of your personality as possible. While the other essay topics focus on leadership, achievement, and personal development, the optional essay affords you an opportunity to enhance your image as an interesting individual or to provide an insight into your unique circumstances. It is a chance to tell a story about something important to you, express a fundamental belief that guides you in everyday life or explain how your commitment to extracurricular activities in college adversely affected your GPA. If there is something meaningful about you that was not conveyed elsewhere, use this opportunity. On the other hand, be sure to avoid repetition. Simply adding volume with no substance is unlikely to improve the overall quality of your application, and may actually detract from it. Also, if you are addressing a less-than-stellar GMAT score, make sure you provide an explanation, not excuses.

In reality, only a handful of applicants include an optional essay. The four following examples included demonstrate the breadth of topics that can be addressed. They all have one thing in common, however; each essay makes you think: "The author must be an interesting person. I would love to meet him or her." If you think your optional essay could elicit this reaction, then by all means include it. Just remember that ultimately what you are doing is trying to strengthen your image as an MBA candidate.

—Pawel Swiatek

Anonymous

At the age of seven, I left my "kid days" of playing banker behind to open a lemonade stand on the front porch. Capitalizing on my parents' planned garage sale, I sold cold drinks and red licorice to the visiting bargain hunters. As the years passed, my ventures evolved into neighborhood car washes and a business called PUPS (personalized urban puppy sitters).

More than a young entrepreneurial instinct, I attribute my actions to the set of values I was imbued with by my parents. They succeeded in teaching me the importance of work and the value of money. While my friends received flat allowances of $20 a week, my sister and I received none. When I begged for the latest gimmicky toy, my mother said "save up your money and buy it." Sure enough, after I had saved enough to purchase a Nintendo set in the fifth grade, I was overflowing with pride. Granted, my sister and I only had enough money for one game, but we played it with relish.

At the age of eleven, I became an avid babysitter, filling my nights, weekends, and even early mornings with child-care commitments. By the time I took off for my junior year in Spain, I had enough savings to cover my personal expenses for the entire year abroad. Churros tasted sweeter and movies were more enjoyable remembering the work that afforded those luxuries.

In university, while taking full loads to complete two bachelor's degrees, I held down several part-time jobs to help support myself through college (working from fifteen to twenty-five hours per week). This, on top of holding multiple club leadership positions and squeezing in time at the gym or with friends, caused friends to question how I fit life into twenty-four-hour days. But work has never been an optional item for me. Though my parents never demanded it, they have taught me why it is indispensable. And it has made me a more independent and disciplined individual.

ANALYSIS

In the context of the other essay topics, it might be difficult to explain how the author of this essay became hardworking, independent, and disciplined. The subject matter is not exactly a defining moment, nor does it easily qualify as one of the three greatest accomplishments. Nonetheless, it effectively illustrates the author's everyday work ethic, as well as its origins.

At first glance, stories about selling soda and babysitting might appear banal, but the author clearly explains how those experiences played a formative role in her personal development. While the other essays in her application most likely describe an accomplished young businesswoman, this one affords a glimpse of how she got there. In this sense, the essay rounds out the application and allows the admissions committee to get to know the author on a more personal level.

ANONYMOUS

I enjoy never giving up, always thinking there's a way, and if there is not one, creating it. I enjoy walking through Central Park with Paige, my girlfriend of six years, and discovering new paths. I enjoy helping Ground Zero construction workers by cold-calling major insole distributors and organizing five hundred pairs of insoles to be donated to the Red Cross. I enjoy seeing that the elevator has not moved off my floor between the time I come home late and when I wake up early to go running the next morning.

I enjoy having close friends with not-so-close personalities, histories, goals, and lifestyles. I have friends who work at Lehman and Solomon, and another who works at her mother's Common Grounds coffee shop; I have friends who visit families on opposite sides of the Dead Sea but can still have peaceful conversations about U.S. foreign policy.

I enjoy never having a single regret, standing in the present and leaning toward the future. I enjoy making mistakes and realizing my first impression was wrong. The best manager I ever worked for initially struck me as a timid and uninspiring person. Weeks later I realized how her unthreatening nature was an incredibly powerful tool in putting clients at ease with changing their minds and with accepting her bold and innovative ideas.

I enjoy listening, learning, trying new things, and growing. I enjoy finally learning to surf Costa Rica's fifteen-foot waves after spending the better part of two days underwater. I enjoy seeing my first boss finally laugh when I built up the nerve to do an impression of her at the company Christmas party. I enjoy laughing, making people laugh, and people that can laugh at themselves.

I enjoy how my family's diversity has shaped me. My younger brother, who spent time in three different high schools, is beginning to act on my coaching that straightening up his act does not mean living an uninteresting life. While my father grew up playing stick-ball on the streets of Queens, N.Y., my mother learned how to sail her father's boat in the Lake of Lucerne in Switzerland. I enjoy my parents' different renditions of my childhood. I enjoy knowing that my personality lies, like the truth in their contrasting tales, some-where in between.

ANALYSIS

As an essay intended to supplement a business school application with personal details, this effort is a tour de force. Every sentence conveys something new about the author—about his interests, feelings, hobbies, and cultural identity. His insatiable appetite for life is impossible to ignore. The seemingly endless list of details, when taken as a whole, paints a picture of a fascinating and com-plex individual. The essay is unassuming and unpretentious, while its honesty makes it instantly credible.

Much like the preceding example, the essay adds tremendous depth to the application. The driven banker becomes a candidate with a very broad and balanced view of the world, able to con-tribute to his MBA community not just a finance skill set, but a deep perspective on happy living.

CABIN KIM

Their dramatic peaks and graceful curves speak volumes.

Chinese characters are expressive, beautiful, deep. Chinese "words" are pictures of ideas, communicating a concept as both what it is and is not. For instance, the character for *man* joins a farmer's field with an arm of strength; to the Chinese, a male without vocation is not truly a man. My life is not just about who I am, but also who I am not. Back in high school, I was an accomplished cellist. But I harbored no illusions about music as a profession, and college life beckoned for my time. I am no longer that cellist; recently, as I played in a trio for a wedding, the violinist repeatedly winced at my good intentions.

Halfway through college, I found myself envying my roommate for his drawing class assignments—I was starving for creative expression. After tasting southern China during a summer Christian mission, I registered for a Chinese class. I was forewarned by Chinese friends who had taken Mandarin at Duke: they, from Chinese-language homes, could barely handle the workload . . . why should I, lacking Chinese background, risk my schedule or my transcript? But life encompasses not just what I choose, but also what I avoid. How could I retreat from the challenge of Chinese before the first day of class?

My three semesters of Chinese were a delight. For hours at a stretch, I hid in the library to write characters, millennia of culture and wisdom flowing through my hand.

I chose to embrace the beauty, expression, and depth of the Chinese language, and the fruit of my choice has become a part of me.

ANALYSIS

While the preceding essay presents an almost overwhelming breadth of experience, Cabin focuses on a single interest. The point, however, is not so much his diligent study of the Chinese language and calligraphy, but rather the philosophical question of choosing challenges in life. The anecdotes demonstrate Cabin's ability to decide which battles are simply not worth fighting. A sense of deep self-awareness permeates the text and implicitly attests to his maturity and poise.

It may seem that this essay has nothing to do with business at all. However, Cabin's introspective skill is likely to be instrumental in his future decision-making in a corporate context. In a very subtle and elegant way, Cabin strengthens his image as a qualified future business leader.

PEDRO RAMOS

I believe it would be helpful for the board if I could share my vision of "social responsibility of individuals."

I believe everyone has the responsibility of putting his/her personal and professional skills to the benefit of the society he/she lives in. To work on behalf of society is to invest in people believing one can make the difference both in the present and in the future world. This responsibility stems from the fact that what we are today has been the product of other people's past investment.

Throughout my life I've always tried to make the difference in my community. I've led a Catholic informal training and development organization for youth, I've visited an orphans' house once a week for a year striving to help them in their personal development, and I've created and currently lead the choir of my community Sunday mass. This is unusual in Portugal since in this country, unlike in the United States, participating in community activities is not a part of common individuals' lives.

I intend to keep on using my skills and forces on community service, either on my free time or while working.

Because of my interest in social activities I admire HBS involvement in social enterprise. Its elective courses, like effective leadership of social enterprises and entrepreneurship in the social sector, its Volunteer Consulting Organization and Social Enterprise Club would make it easier for someone like me to be actively involved in social enterprises activities throughout my life.

ANALYSIS

Pedro uses the optional essay to share a very strong opinion about people's social responsibilities. While running the risk of sounding a little dogmatic, he successfully describes one of the driving forces in his life. Lest it be viewed as abstract and unrealistic, Pedro backs up his convictions with specific examples of community involvement.

Pedro's text is a good example of using the optional essay to strengthen an application. He clearly connects his very deep commitment to community service with HBS's social enterprise program and the Volunteer Consulting Organization. In effect, he demonstrates that not only is he very familiar with the school, but also his values are very much aligned with those of HBS, which makes him a "natural" candidate.